Songs of Tagore

Songs of Tagore

Selection and translation: **Aruna Chakravarti**
Foreword: **Sunil Gangopadhyay**

NIYOGI
BOOKS

Published by
NIYOGI BOOKS
D-78, Okhla Industrial Area, Phase-I
New Delhi-110 020, INDIA
Tel: 91-11-26816301, 49327000
Fax: 91-11-26810483, 26813830
email: niyogibooks@gmail.com
website: www.niyogibooks.com

Editor: Mohua Mitra/Niyogi Books
Design: Shashi Bhushan Prasad/Niyogi Books

ISBN: 978-93-81523-49-0

Publication: 2012

Printed at: Niyogi Offset Pvt. Ltd., New Delhi, India

To Sudhir Chanda…

for initiating me into the mysteries of Rabindrasangeet.

The poet with nephew Abanindranath, c 1888-89

Contents

Rabindranath Tagore: 1861-1941

Foreword

Rabindranath Tagore received the Nobel Prize in 1913 for the English version of his *Gitanjali* originally published in Bengali in 1910. Though the translation was undertaken by the poet himself and the two books were given the same title, there are some differences in them. Several additions and deletions are found in the English version.

The Nobel Award for *Gitanjali* surprised and continues to surprise critics and scholars. Some of Rabindranath's best poetry collections such as *Manasi, Sonar Tari* and *Chitra* had appeared prior to *Gitanjali.* If one were to conduct a comparative evaluation of the poems of the earlier anthologies with those of *Gitanjali,* there is no doubt that the latter would appear somewhat feeble. One wonders why Rabindranath chose to translate, for his foreign readers, the poems of *Gitanjali,* actually a collection of songs, in preference to the ones which, in terms of poetic excellence, were far superior. Could it be because Europe at that time, stood on the brink of a devastating world war and its people were staggering under a load of anxiety and depression? Did Rabindranath feel that, at such a juncture, readers were not in a mood for intellectually stimulating poetry? That they would prefer the refreshing, spiritually optimistic verses of *Gitanjali* which soothed the mind and brought peace to the soul? In all probability that was the reasoning behind the choice of *Gitanjali.*

Rabindranath chose an archaic form of English for his translation, something like the language of the *Bible.* That, perhaps, was an added attraction. Even Yeats and Ezra Pound, who used a robust, modern English for their own poetry, declared themselves spell-bound by the oriental poet's quaint, old fashioned expressions. The euphoria, however, was short lived. A few years later Yeats started taking an active dislike to both Rabindranath's language and his spiritualism so much so that he instructed the publisher to refrain from publishing the Indian poet's other works.

We, who have read the original *Gitanjali,* do not appreciate the translated version. When Rabindranath wrote in his mother tongue he used the living language; a Bengali that, in his hands, became more vigorous and expressive with each new effort. Why did he choose a dead, archaic medium for his English translation?

There have been several other attempts at rendering the poems of *Gitanjali* into English since Rabindranath's own but not one has proved worthwhile. The reason for this, obviously, is that translating poetry is a far more demanding task than translating prose. Translating songs is even more difficult, well nigh impossible. Rabindranath often composed the music first and incorporated the words later. The translator should be able to infuse the translation with the rhythm and cadence of the original composition. But that is easier said than done. Translators in general, learn the source language and carry the poem over into English in ordinary prose, missing out the finer, delicate nuances of the original Bengali. I'll give an example. An eminent Western translator used the word 'prisoner' as an English equivalent for *bandi* in one of his translations. But though one English equivalent of the word is, indeed, 'prisoner' the word in the original poem stood for *bandanakari* or 'the one who sings a song of praise or salutation'. That this was Rabindranath's intended meaning is obvious in the context in which the word is found—'*bandi raa dhorey shondhyaar taan*'–which means that the *bandi*s start singing an evening raga. The use of the word 'prisoner' is totally out of context here.

Aruna Chakravarti's mother tongue is Bengali and the language of her education–English. She has a fine grasp of both languages and understands their subtleties and cultural nuances. She has received a number of awards for her translations but mostly for her prose work. These days one doesn't see her translating poetry. Yet in her first publication, she displayed the rare courage of translating some of Rabindranath's songs into English.

In this connection I would like to narrate a personal experience. About twenty-five years ago the editors of a popular journal *The Illustrated Weekly of India* wished to interview me for one of their issues. They sent a photographer who took me around to several places in Kolkata and clicked a number of pictures. One of them was to show me reclining in a boat on the Ganga reading a book. My table was littered with books sent by various publishers which I hadn't even opened. I picked up one at random and got ready. It was a translation of some lyrics of Rabindranath by one Aruna Chakravarti. I hadn't even heard of her at that time. I opened the book and carelessly, half heartedly, I read the first poem. I sat up startled. The translation was so natural and spontaneous that the shift from Bengali to English was hardly perceptible. And I felt as though I could hear the primary tune and rhythm of the original. I read a few more and my amazement grew. Over the next two days, I read the book at home again and again.

Aruna writes in English but knows her Bengali well. She also sings Rabindrasangeet—an advantage other translators may not have. I'm sure she hums the lines to herself while translating. That is how she gives her renderings an added dimension. I do not know if any other translation of Rabindranath's songs have matched hers in authenticity.

The book has been out of print for many years now. I'm very happy that another, revised edition with some more inclusions is being published on the occasion of the 150th birth anniversary of Rabindranath. I have no doubt that, among the innumerable books that are seeing the light of day on this occasion, this one will find a prominent place.

Sunil Gangopadhyay
April, 2012

Translator's Note

Culled from our great poet and composer Rabindranath Tagore's vast repository these English renderings of 112 lyrics have been created and compiled at the request of non-resident Indians as well as non-Bengali-speaking admirers of the poet who often hear the songs and appreciate their tunes and rhythms but, being somewhat unfamiliar with the language, remain unaware of the poet's profound philosophy of life, his sensitive exploration of the Universe and his enduring faith in humanity—all of which find expression in his lyrics. For Rabindrasangeet, in its innermost essence, is a unique combination of poetry and melody that has captured the sensibilities of generations of Indians and continues to do so both at home and abroad.

The poet composed, in all, 2200 songs—surpassingly beautiful creations that drew from the famous Bengali film maker, Satyajit Ray, the comment, 'as a composer of songs, Tagore has no equal, not even in the West.' ('Some Reflections on Rabindrasangeet', *Purabi: A Miscellany in Memory of Rabindranath Tagore, p 177*)

The songs that I have chosen for translation constitute a representative cross-section of the collection. They are much loved and often sung. Ranging in theme from prayer and love to nature and nationalism they often touch on the quest of the elusive, intangible and unattainable. Rabindranath once said that, though he could not predict for certain how future generations would receive his work; that he was afraid much of it would gradually pass into oblivion—he was confident that his songs would live. The increasing popularity of Rabindrasangeet, the world over, bears testimony to the fact that his prophecy was based on a certainty born out of self knowledge. Vast and varied though his genius was, music was its mainspring. 'I feel as if music wells up from within some unconscious depth of my being', he said to an admirer once, 'and that is why it has a certain completeness.'

Rabindranath started writing songs and setting them to music from his boyhood. His much-acclaimed composition *Jwol jwol chitaa dwigun dwigun* ('Burn pyre burn, leap doublefold'—pg 124) was written at the age of fifteen and presented by him as a surprise offering to his brother Jyotirindranath for the *jawahar vrat* scene of the play *Sarojini*. In the years that followed, Rabindranath wrote devotional songs for the Brahmo Samaj and romantic songs for family weddings and celebrations. Then, drawn by his sister-in-law Kadambari into the mystic, alluring world of the Vaishnav versifiers, he composed the lyrics later compiled in the volume *Bhanu Singher Padavali*. These early beginnings sparked off a career spanning more than six decades reaching its culmination in the publication of *Gitanjali*, an anthology of 157 devotional songs written in 1910. Two years later 103 lyrics – most of them from the original *Gitanjali* and some culled from other collections – were translated into English by the poet himself. This English version was awarded the Nobel Prize for literature in 1913—the first ever to an Asian and the only one of its genre to an Indian till date.

Making music came naturally to Rabindranath. Tutors, proficient in North Indian classical music, were employed by his father to train the young scions of the family. Though Rabindranath was not an apt pupil as a child – his tutors complained that he paid scant attention – he had an innate ability to assimilate and sustain all the cultural activity that went on around him. He absorbed music, easily and spontaneously, and made it his own. Fusion and experimental modes came naturally to him. At the age of seventeen, during a brief sojourn in England, he heard Irish and Scottish melodies and was so enchanted by them that he used some of the tunes, sometimes blending them with indigenous ones.

Another strong inspiration came from Baul music. As a youth of twenty he was sent by his father to supervise the collection of rents from the family estates in the eastern part of Bengal, now Bangladesh. It was here that he heard a Baul sing for the first time. The song was *Aami kothaay paabo taarey aamaar moner maanush jey rey*—'Where shall I find him? / He who is the man of my heart' – and the singer was a postal runner by the name of Gagan Harkara. This song (he used the melody for his famous *Aamaar shonaar baanglaa aami tomaay bhaalobaashi* – 'My golden Bengal/I love you' – now the national anthem of Bangladesh) made a lasting impact on young Rabindranath. He began seeking out Bauls and hearing their songs. Fascinated by their rustic tunes and profound philosophy of life, he began introducing Baul thought and melody into his own compositions. 'In some songs,' he tells

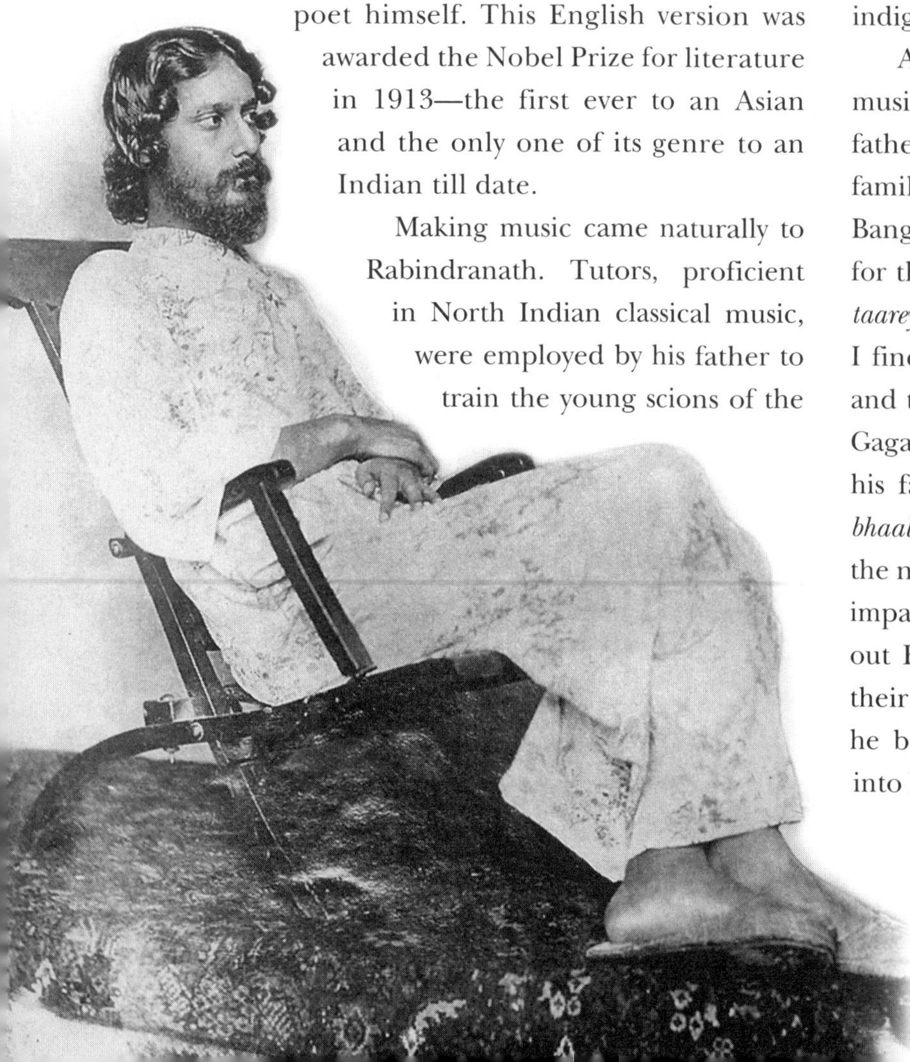

Tagore at Silaidaha, 1890

us in his *Manusher dharma* (Rabindra Rachanabali vol 20. p 380) 'the primary tunes got mixed up with other raag raaginis which prove that the Baul idiom had entered my subconscious.'

'The *Upanishads*,' he wrote many years later in his Preface to *Haramoni* (vol 2. ed. Muhammud Mansooruddin) 'speak of the one who dwells deep within the heart – the *antartama hridyatma* – and the Baul sings of the *moner manush.* They seem to me to be one and the thought fills me with wonder. What I heard from the mouth of a peasant in a rustic dialect and a primary tune was the same.' In the last half of his life he experimented with other musical forms—Keertan, Carnatic music, Christian hymns, Sikh Shabad and many others. In the process a brilliant new genre of Indian music evolved. Rabindrasangeet came into being.

In 1931 Rabindranath compiled his lyrics in two volumes according to their dates of composition. Later, in the last years of his life, he took on the arduous task of classifying them according to theme. Six sections were formed—*Puja, Prem, Swadesh, Prakriti, Bichitra* and *Anushthanik* namely *Songs of Devotion, Love, Motherland, Nature, Variegated Songs* and *Songs for Ceremonial Occasions.* The anthology also contained the lyrics he had composed for his musicals and dance dramas. Due to failing health he was unable to complete his undertaken task. But in 1942, a year after his death, the reworked anthology was published under the title *Gitabitan.*

The songs selected for this volume follow the same classification and sequence. But only the first five sections are represented. The sixth, *Anushthanik* or *Ceremonial Songs,* has been left out for no other reason than a dilemma of choice. There are only seventeen songs in this section but they cover a broad spectrum of events ranging from compositions for Brahmo Samaj meetings, National Conferences, weddings and funerals, to Visva-Bharati convocations and the poet's own birthdays.

And now a few words about my translation. Translation is the only way we have of disseminating gems from the literature of one culture to another and the wider the reach of the target language the better the dissemination. Thus the choice of English. But the greater the divergence between the source and target literary traditions the greater is the skill required to bring them together in a meaningful way. Mediating between the reader's expectations and the authenticity of the chosen text demands great sensibility as well as close monitoring, the aim being to acquire the finest balance possible between the two. When the translation is of Rabindrasangeet and the target language English, the difficulties grow a hundred fold. Tagore's lyrics are characterised by a strange compound of nostalgia, ecstasy and despair which flow as much from the words of the poem as from the music of the composition. In translating them I set myself the formidable task of retaining their haunting aura and sounds as well as their primary tunes and rhythms. But how was I to do it? Forcing a rhyming pattern would certainly lead to deviations from the original. I had to look for alternate devices. I went,

I confess, totally by instinct. What sounded right in my ears, *was* right, I felt. I'll give some examples. The song *Mon mor megher shongi* (pg 86) relies on repetitive use of alliteration and onomatopoeia to capture the sounds of rain and thunder. I tried to reproduce these effects using the same techniques in English. In another poem *Shudhu jaaoaa aashaa shudhu srotey bhaashaa* (pg 136) I employed a tetrametric division of lines which echo the original in swing and rhyme. In another song *Himer raatey oi gogoner deep guli rey* (pg 106) I rendered the opening line as 'On a dewy night of November', there being no season in the English cycle that corresponds exactly, in its literary and sentimental associations, to the Bengali season of Hemanta.

A hundred songs from the present collection had appeared earlier in a volume entitled *Tagore: Songs Rendered into English* in 1984. However the present collection is not a mere copy of the earlier volume. After all, more than twenty-five years have passed since, the world has grown older and our understanding of Tagore has also undergone changes. A re-look has been taken at the earlier translations as well, which are being published as new offerings. The earlier publication was undertaken by a Mumbai–based organisation called *Vaitalik* which sought to bring about appreciation and understanding between people of diverse linguistic groups through music and art. It was released by Mrs Indira Gandhi, then Prime Minister of India, in April 1984, a few months before her assassination. I owe a deep debt of gratitude to her.

I would also like to take this opportunity to reiterate my thanks to the Executive Members of *Vaitalik* (many of whom are no more) for sanctioning the grants and bringing out the earlier volume which was to launch me on my writing career. Today, nearly three decades later, this revised edition with substantial new inputs, is about to see the light of day. I'm indebted to Bikash and Tultul De Niyogi of Niyogi Books for undertaking this publication and to Nirmal Kanti Bhattacharjee for recommending it. My heartfelt thanks to eminent writer Sunil Gangopadhyay for writing the Foreword and, last though not least, my deepest gratitude to the editor Mohua Mitra for her meticulous and reader-friendly transliterations of the original Bangla songs into the Roman script.

—Aruna Chakravarti
July, 2012

Songs of Devotion

YA MAR BE - LA - J - JA - -
- YA SA NJ BE - LA - TE -
O MA R SU - RE - - SU - RE -
-- - - SU R ME - LA - TE - -

Mohaabishwe mohaakaashey mohaakaal maajhey
aami maanob ekaaki bhromi bishmoye, bhromi bishmoye.
Tumi aachho, bishwonaath, osheem rohoshyomaajhey
neerobey ekaaki aapon mohimaaniloye.
Ononto e desh kaaley, ogonyo e deepto lokey,
Tumi aachho morey chaahi—aami chaahi tomaa-paaney.
Stobdho shorbo kolaahol, shaantimogno choraachor—
Ek tumi, tomaa-maajhey aami ekaa nirbhoye.

Rapt in wonder, a common man
I wander alone in the vast expanse
of the firmament of shining stars;
through all eternity.

You are, oh Lord of the universe
shrouded in veils of mystery;
the soul of silence, alone, apart
in your abode of glory.

Eternal in space and time;
infinite in this vault of light,
your gaze is fixed upon my soul
and my eyes upon your face.

When the din and bustle ceases,
peace dawns upon the sphere;
when all else is naught in the searing light
of your invisible form...

then, though in desolation,
with courage and with faith,
Only one, through eternal life
I shall exist in you.

Gaaner bhitor diye jokhon dekhi bhubonkhaani
Tokhon taarey chini aami, tokhon taarey jaani.
Tokhon taari aalor bhaashaay aakaash bhorey bhaalobaashaay,
Tokhon taari dhulaay dhulaay jaagey porom baani.
Tokhon shey jey baahir chherey ontorey more aashey,
Tokhon aamaar hridoy kaanpey taari ghaashey ghaashey.
Ruper rekhaa rosher dhaaraay aapon sheemaa kothaay haaraay,
Tokhon dekhi aamaar shaathey shobaar kaanaakaani.

When through music
the world comes within my vision;
I see Him.
I know Him.

Then through the language of His radiance,
the sky is filled with love.
Each fragment of dust is awakened
and speaks a golden word.

It is then that He ceases to be an outsider
and enters into my very being;
and my heart trembles
with every blade of grass.

Then the lines of all visible forms
are washed away in a flood of nectar;
and I can hear the murmur
of all created things.

Aamaar mukti aloye aloye ei aakaashey,
Aamaar mukti dhulaay dhulaay ghaashey ghaashey.
Deho moner shudoor paarey haariye pheli aaponaarey,
Gaaner shurey aamaar mukti oordhey bhaashey.
Aamar mukti shorbojoner moner maajhey,
Dukkho bipod-tuchho koraa kothin kaajey.
Bishwadhaataar jogyoshaalaa aatmohomer bohni jwaalaa—
Jibon jano di-i ahooti mukti-aashey.

I am released into the light,
in this sky.
I am merged with each fragment of dust;
with every blade of grass.

Beyond the horizons of mind and body
I lose myself.
To the strains of music,
my disembodied soul
floats higher and higher.

My release is in the minds of men;
in the hard labour that scorns pain and peril.

In the temple of the Creator;
into the scorching flames of self sacrifice,
may my life be dedicated,
in the hope of salvation.

Tomaay aamaay milon hobey bo'ley
aaloy aakaash bhoraa.
Tomaay aamaay milon hobey bo'ley phullo shyaamol dhoraa.
Tomaay aamaay milon hobey bo'ley raatri jaagey jogot loye koley,
Ushaa eshey poorbo dooaar kholey kolokonthoshworaa.
Cholchhey bheshey milon-aashaa-tori onaadi srote beye.
Koto kaaler kushum uthey bhori borondaali chheye.
Tomaay aamaay milon hobey bo'ley
jugey jugey bishwo bhubon toley
Poraan aamaar bodhoor beshey choley chiroshoyomboraa.

The sky is flooded with light
because we two shall meet.
The green earth springs with blossom,
because we two shall meet.
Because we two shall meet
the night keeps awake with the earth in her lap.

Dawn opens the doors of the east
with a joyful call;
the bark of the hope of union
sails down the eternal stream.
Many a timeless flower fills the basket of welcome,
because we two shall meet.

Through aeons of time in the boundless universe,
a blushing bride in gorgeous bridal raiment
my soul goes forth on an eternal quest,
to seek the lord of love.

Modhur, tomaar shesh jey naa paai prohor holo shesh—
Bhubon jurey roilo legey aanondo-aabesh.
Dinaanter ei ek konaatey shondhyaa megher ek shonaatey
Mon jey aamaar gunjorichhey kothaay niruddesh.
Shaayontoner klaanto phuler gondho haaoaar 'porey
Ongo biheen aalingoney shokol ongo bhorey.
Ei godhoolir dhooshorimaay shyaamol dhoraar sheemaay sheemaay
Shuni boney bonaantorey osheem gaaner resh.

Boundless is your loveliness; infinite, eternal!
Over the earth though the day is almost done,
a languorous bliss, a tender indolence
remains; still touching, softly clinging.

At wane of day I sit in my lonely corner,
watching the last streaks of gold on evening clouds;
my heart murmuring in song,
'where, oh! where lies that alien land?'

At dusk, when weary flowers
have yielded their scent upon the air,
an embrace, unfelt, unseen,
enters my heart, suffusing all my limbs.

Now as gathering twilight creeps slowly
over the horizon,
casting dark shadows on the emerald earth,
I hear from meadow, glade and forest,
echoes of a song eternal.

Tumi jey shurer aagun laagiye diley more praaney,
e aagun chhoriye galo shob khaaney.
Joto shob moraa gaachher daaley daaley
naachey aagun taaley taaley rey,
Aakaashey haat toley shey kaar paaney.
Aandhaarer taaraa joto obaak hoye roy cheye,
Kothaakaar paagol haaoaa boy dheye.
Nisheether buker maajhey ei-jey omol
uthlo phutey shworno-komol rey,
Aagooner ki goon aachhey ke jaaney.

You have set the fire of music burning in my soul
and the blaze has spread in all directions.

Flames leap merrily from branch to branch
of all the dead trees,
dancing in rhythm,
shooting up to touch the sky.
Whom do they hope to reach,
those flaming fingers?

The twilight stars look on in wonder;
a gust of wind, like one possessed,
goes roaring past.
In the bosom of the night
a golden lotus is born;
its petals pure and bright.
Who knows what magic is hidden
in this fire you have kindled?

Aami tomaay joto shuniyechhilem gaan
Taar bodoley aami chaai ney kono daan.
Bhulbey shey gaan jodi naa hoy jeyo bhuley
Uthbey jokhon taaraa shondhyaa shaagor kooley,
Tomaar shobhaay jobey korbo oboshaan
Ei kodiner shudhu ei koti more taan.
Tomaar gaan jey koto shuniyechhiley morey
shei kothaati tumi bhulbey kamon korey?
Shei kothaati, kobi, porbey tomaar money
borshaamukhor raatey, phaagun-shomironey—
Ei tuku more shudhu roilo obhimaan
Bhultey shey ki paaro bhuliyechho more praan.

I have sung many songs for you
but asked for no return.
If your memory holds them no longer
I will not question why.

When the star of the evening rises
on the shore of the twilit sea,
when I fade away from your gathering;
when I cease to be ...

then these few strains of melody
the fruits of a life time's care,
I shall offer to you my lord
upon the darkening air.

You have sung many songs for me.
How can you help but remember?
They will come to your mind oh poet!
on rain washed monsoon eves ...

and the sweet breezes of springtime.
Yet my wounded spirit murmurs ...
Can you forget the one whose soul
you've lured away with song?

Tomaar ei maadhuri chhaapiye aakaash jhorbey,
Aamaar praaney noiley shey ki kothaao dhorbey?
Ei-jey aalo shoorjye grohey taaraay
jhorey porey shoto lokkho dhaaraay,
Poorno hobey e praan jokhon bhorbey.
Tomaar phuley jey rong ghoomer moto laaglo
Aamar money legey tobey shey jey jaaglo go.
Jey prem kaanpaaye bishwobeenay pulokey shongeetey shey
uthbey bheshey polokey
jey din aamaar shokol hridoy horbey.

This loveliness of yours must flood the sky
and rain upon my heart,
for in the void there is not space enough
to hold that mighty stream.

This light that falls in multi-myriad beams
upon the sun, the planets and the stars,
will fill the spheres the day it fills my life,
full to the brim, with radiance.

The hues that touch your flowers like sweet sleep
caress my soul, then wake in ecstasy.
Love, quivering on the lyre of life in tremulous delight
will float in song upon your eyes,
the day my heart is won.

Aamaar belaa jey jaaye shaanjh-belaatey
tomaar shurey shurey shur melaatey.
Ektaaraatir ekti taarey gaaner bedon boitey naarey,
Tomaar shaathey baarey baarey haar menechhi ei khelaatey
tomaar shurey shurey shur melaatey.
E taar baandhaa kaachher shurey,
Oi baanshi jey baajey doorey.
Gaaner leelaay shei kinaarey joge ditey ki shobaai paarey
Bishwohridoy paaraabaarey raag raaginir jaal phelaatey—
tomaar shurey shurey shur melaatey.

My day wanes in the twilight gloaming,
singing in tune to your melody,
but the lone string of my instrument
bears not the anguish of my song.
I lose each time to you, my friend,
in this game we play together.

My single string can only strum
an air of here and now.
Your flute bursts forth with strains divine
in a land of no return.

Ah! can I reach the distant shore
of the universal ocean
and in its heart cast forth the net
of cosmic symphony?
Thus I waste the long, long day
singing in tune to your melody.

Jibon moroner sheemaanaa chharaaye,
bondhu hey aamaar, royechho daanraaye.
E more hridoyer bijon aakaashey
tomaar mohaashon aalotey dhaakaa shey,
gobheer ki aashaay nibir pulokey
taahaar paaney chaai du baahu baaraaye.
Neerob nishi tobo choron nichhaaye
aandhaar-keshbhaar diyechhey bichhaye.
Aaji e kon gaan nikhil plaabiyaa
tomaar beenaa haatey aashilo naabiyaa
Bhubon miley jaaye shurer roroney,
gaaner bedonaay jaai jey haaraaye.

Beyond the horizons of life and death,
you are waiting, my friend,
in the desolate sky of my heart.

Your mighty throne is hidden from my vision
by the radiance of your presence;
still in secret joy and throbbing hope,
I stretch out my arms to you.

The silent night has spread
its dark tresses at your feet.
From your divine lyre
what melody wells forth,
flooding the Universe?
The earth trembles in ecstasy
at those shattering chords,
and I am lost in the agony of your song.

Aamaar maathaa noto korey daao hey
tomaar chorono dhoolaar toley.
Shokolo ohonkaar hey aamaar dubaao chokher joley.
Nijerey koritey gourob daan nijerey keboli kori opomaan,
Aaponaarey shudhu gheriyaa gheriyaa ghurey mori poley poley.
Shokol ohonkaar hey aamaar dubaao chokher joley.
Aamaarey naa jano kori prochaar aamaar aapon kaajey,
Tomaari ichhaa koro hey poorno aamaar jibonmaajhey.
Jaachi hey tomaar chorom shaanti,
poraaney tomaar poromkaanti—
Aamaarey aaraal koriyaa daanraao hridoy poddodoley
Shokol ohonkaar hey aamaar dubaao chokher joley.

Bow down my head oh! Lord
beneath the dust of your feet.
Drown all my pride in streaming tears.

In the seeking of self glory,
I only abuse myself.
I waste each waking moment
spinning around
a pin point that is I.

In my work may my image be not projected.
In the stream of my life may your will be fulfilled!

From you I seek only everlasting peace,
your beauteous face embossed upon my soul.
Come, stand upon the lotus of my heart oh! Lord
and hide me behind your presence.

Daako morey aaji e nisheethey nidraamogon jobey bishwojogot,
Hridoye aashiye nirobey daako hey tomaari omritey.
Jwaalo tobo deep e ontortimirey,
Baar baar daako momo ocheto chitey.

Call out to me my Lord, now on this night
when the world is wrapped in slumber.

Come close to my heart and whisper,
Come ... enter my sea of nectar.

Light your lamp in the darkness of my being
calling again and again,
striking my unconscious soul
with the sombre ringing of your voice.

More hridoyer gopon bijon ghorey
akelaa royechho neerob shoyon'porey—
Priyotomo hey, jaago jaago jaago.
Ruddho dwaarer baahirey daanraaye aami
aar kotokaal emon kaatibey shwaami—
priyotomo hey, jaago jaago jaago.
Rojonir taaraa uthechhey gogon chheye,
aachhey shob more baataayon-paaney cheye—
priyotomo hey, jaago jaago jaago.
Jeeboney aamaar shongeet daao aani,
neerob rekho naa tomaar beenaar baani
priyotomo hey, jaago jaago jaago.
Milaabo noyon tobo noyoner shaathey,
milaabo e haat tobo dokkhin haatey—
priyotomo hey, jaago jaago jaago
Hridoy paatro shudhaay poorno hobey,
timir kaanpibey gobheer aalor robey—
priyotomo hey, jaago jaago jaago.

In the secret closet of my heart,
you lie in solitary slumber.
Awake, beloved ... awake!

How much longer shall I stand
waiting outside your door?
Awake, beloved ... awake!

The stars of the night spread across the sky,
gaze into my casement.
Awake, beloved ... awake!

Keep not your divine lyre mute of words.
Let the strains of your music
fill the vessel of my life
full to the brim with nectar.
Awake, beloved ... awake!

I shall clasp your hands with trembling fingers;
my eyes will gaze into yours.
The dark night will tremble
with the explosion of your radiance.
Awake, beloved ... awake!

Daanriye aachho tumi aamaar gaaner opaarey—
Aamaar shurguli paay choron, aami paai ne tomaarey.
Baataash bohey mori mori, aar bendhey rekho naa tori—
esho esho paar hoye more hridoymaajhaarey.
Tomaar shaathey gaaner khelaa doorer khelaa jey,
bedonaa tey baanshi baajaay shokol belaa jey.
Kobey niye aamaar baanshi baajaabey go aapni aashi
aanondomoy neerob raater nibir aandhaarey.

You stand on the other bank
of the stream of my flowing song.
My melodies lap your feet
but my heart is not borne along.

The breeze ripples like a gentle murmur;
keep your boat tied no more—
come, cross the stream and enter
the vault of my inmost soul.

I play a singing game with you
but the game is of far away.
In poignant pain I raise my flute
to my lips the livelong day.

When will you take my flute away
and pipe sweet tunes for me?
In the deep dark of a silent night;
in the joy of tranquility.

Kool thekey more gaaner toree dilem khuley,
Shaagor-maajhey bhaashiye dilem paalti tuley.
Jekhaaney oi kokil daakey chhaayaatoley shekhaaney noy,
Jekhaaney oi graamer bodhoo, aashey joley shekhaaney noy,
Jekhaaney neel moronoleela uthchhey duley
shekhaaney more gaaner toree dilem khuley.
Ebaar, beenaa, tomaay aamaay aamraa ekaa—
ondhokaarey naaibaa kaarey galo dekhaa
Kunjoboner shaakhaa hotey jey phul toley
shey phuley noy,
baataayoner lotaa hotey jey phul doley
shey phuley noy—
Dishaahaaraa aakaash-bhoraa shurer phuley
Shei dikey more gaaner toree dilem khuley.

I have loosened the bark of my song from the shore,
hoisted the sail and set it afloat
upon the wide, wide sea.

Not where the cuckoo sings sweetly in the shade,
not where the village bride stands by the water,
but there, where in the blue ocean
the rearing waves play the game of death;
there, I set sail the bark of my song.

Now we are alone, you and I, my lyre.
It matters not, if all else is invisible
in the gathering dusk.

Not for me the bloom plucked from the branch
of a flowering tree
in a shadowy bower.
Not for me the blossom swinging coyly from a creeper
trailing the casement;
but there where the boundless sky
is showered with flowers of melody;
there, I set sail the bark of my song.

Probhu aamaar, priyo aamaar porom dhon hey
Chiropother shongi aamaar chirojeebon hey.
Tripti aamaar, otripti more, mukti aamaar, bondhondore,
Dhukkho shukher chorom-aamaar jeebon moron hey.
Aamaar shokol gotir maajhey porom goti hey
nityo premer dhaamey aamaar poromo poti hey.
Ogo shobaar, ogo aamaar, bishwo hotey chittey bihaar—
Ontobiheen khelaa tomaar nooton nooton hey.

You are my Lord, you are my love,
my prime and priceless treasure;
companion of my endless path,
through eternal life.

You are my peace, my suffering,
my freedom, my life's bonds;
the ultimate in joy and pain,
the last in death and life.

In all my swift progression,
you are the final goal;
oh! perfect Lord of my daily love ...
husband of my soul!

Ah! only mine, ah! everyone's,
all hearts are taken by storm;
in this world by your endless play,
in ever-changing form.

Aaji naahi naahi nidraa aankhipaatey.
Tomaar bhobon toley heri prodeep jwoley,
Doorey baahirey timirey aami jaagi jor haatey.
Krondon dhwonichhey poth haaraa poboney,
rojoni moorchhaagoto bidyut ghaatey.
Dwaar kholo hey dwaar kholo—
Probhu, koro doyaa, deho dekhaa dukhoraatey.

Tonight my lids are untouched by slumber.
From afar I see the lamp
burning in your closet,
while I keep vigil in the distant dark,
hands folded in prayer.

The moaning wind is lost in the pathless void.
The deep night swoons as the lightning strikes.
Open your door to the homeless wanderer.
Reveal yourself oh Lord ...
on this dark night of sorrow.

Tomaar shurer dhaaraa jhorey jethaay taari paarey
debey ki go baashaa aamaay ekti dhaarey?
Aami shunbo dhwoni kaaney,
aami bhorbo dhwoni praaney,
Shei dhwonitey chittobinaay taar baandhibo baarey baarey.
Aamaar neerob belaa shei tomaari shurey shurey
phuler bhitor modhur moto uthbey purey.
Aamaar din phuraabey jobey,
jokhon raatri aandhaar hobey,
Hridoye more gaaner taaraa uthbey phutey shaarey shaarey.

Where the stream of your melody comes
gushing forth
will you build me a hut,
in a corner by the bank?

My ears shall be filled with your music;
my heart will echo the same.
To those strains shall I string the lyre of my soul
again and again.

Like the honey dew that fills the breast
of a flower new blown in spring,
on my hour of silence, like drops, shall fall
your gentle symphony.

When my day ends, in the dark of night,
in rows upon my heart
the stars of your song will burst forth and shine
in eternal radiance.

Eki e shundoro shobhaa! ki mukho heri e!
aaji more ghorey aailo hridoy naath,
Prem-utsho utholilo aaji.
Bolo hey premomoy hridoyer shwaami,
ki dhon tomaarey dibo upohaar
Hridoy praan loho loho tumi, ki bolibo—
Jaahaa-kichhu aachhey momo shokoli lao hey naath.

What wondrous beauty!
Whose face is this which I behold?
He who rules my heart has come to my home
and the fountain of love gushes forth.

Speak oh husband! Oh loving lord!
What gift shall I offer you?
My heart, my life, my eternal soul...
ask and they shall be yours.

What shall I say? All... all I have
is yours, is yours, is yours.

Dukkher timirey jodi jwoley tobo mongol-aalok
tobey taai hok.
Mrityu jodi kaachhey aaney tomaar omritomoy lok
tobey taai hok.
Pujaar prodeepey tobo jwoley jodi momo deepto shoke
tobey taai hok.
Osru-aankhi-'porey jodi phutey othey tobo sneho chokh
tobey taai hok.

If your divine light shines forth
on my dark night of sorrow;
so be it.

If death alone brings near
your abode of sweetness;
so be it.

If anguish burns like a flame
in the heart of your sacred lamp;
so be it.

If in the dark pools of my flowing tears
your tender eyes bloom forth;
so be it, my Lord!

Aamaar hiyaar maajhey lukiye chhiley dekhtey aami paaini.
Tomaay dekhtey aami paaini.
Bahir paaney chokh melechhi, aamaar hridoy-paaney chaaini.
Aamaar shokol bhaalobaashaay, shokol aaghaat shokol aashaay
tumi chhiley aamaar kaachhey, tomaar kaachhey jaaini.
Tumi more aanondo hoye chhiley aamaar khelaay—
Aanondey taai bhuley chhilem, ketechhey din helaay.
Gopon rohi gobheer praaney aamaar dukkho shukher gaaney
Shur diyechho tumi, aami tomaar gaan to gaaini.

You lay hidden in my heart
and I could not see you.
My eyes gazed out over the vast exterior;
I looked not into my soul.

In all my love, my hope, my suffering,
you stood by my side
and I turned not towards you.

In the games I played you were my joy;
in joy I forgot you
and the days went by.

Within my soul, in silence, in secret
you lay hidden.
You gave me the melody for all my songs
but I sang not of you.

Shudhu tomaar baani noy go, hey bondhu, hey priyo,
Maajhey maajhey praaney tomaar, porosh khaani diyo.
Shaaraa pother klaanti aamaar shaaraa diner trishaa
Kemon korey metaabo jey khunjey naa paai dishaa—
E aandhaar jey poorno tomaay shei kothaa boliyo.
Hridoy aamaar chaay jey ditey, kebol nitey noy,
Boye boye beraay shey taar jaa-kichhu shonchoy.
Haatkhaani oi baariye aano, daao go aamaar haatey—
dhorbo taarey, bhorbo taarey, raakhbo taarey shaathey,
Aklaa pother cholaa aamaar korbo romoniyo.

Not only your word, my beloved, my friend...
let my soul at moments too
feel the touch of your presence.

I grope in the dark,
not knowing how to quench
the thirst of the day;
how soothe away the weariness
of a long, long path.
Ah! If only you would whisper in my heart,
This darkness is mine.

Weary of receiving, my heart yearns to give.
It carries all day the burden of its savings;
in the hope that someday
you will stretch out your hand,
and, taking it in mine,
I shall fill it and keep it
forever at my breast.
Then the dark hours of my solitary journey
will be suffused with the light of your alluring form.

Tumi kamon korey gaan koro hey guni,
aami obaak hoye shuni kebol shuni.
Shurer aalo bhubon phaley chheye,
Shurer haaoaa choley gogon beye,
paashaan tutey byaakul begey dheye
bohiyaa jaay shurer shurodhuni.
Money kori omni shurey gaai,
konthey aamaar shur khunjey naa paai.
Koitey ki chaai, koitey kothaa baadhey—
Haar meney jey poraan aamaar kaandey,
Aamaay tumi phelechho kon phaandey
Choudikey more shurer jaal buni.

How do you sing oh! Master?
I marvel at your song
while I listen; ever listen.

The radiance of your strains engulfs the earth,
borne across the skies on the wings of winds.
Crushing the rocks in anguished, frenzied spate
flows the mighty Ganga of your song.

I try to match my song with yours
but my voice is bereft of melody.
I try to speak but I find no words
and my heart weeps in the knowledge that I fail.

Ah! What is this snare you have laid for me
weaving around me your web of song?

Dukkhoraatey, hey naath, key daakiley—
Jaagi herinu tobo premmukhochhobi.
Herinu ushaalokey bishwo tobo koley,
jaagey tobo noyoney praatey shubhro robi.
Shuninu boney upoboney aanondogaathaa,
aashaa hridoye bohi nityo gaahey kobi.

On this dark night of sorrow,
whose voice, my Lord
called out my name?
On waking I saw your face
alight with love.

At dawn I beheld you
with the earth in your lap;
and in the morn the silver sun
awake in your eyes.

I heard a poet
sing a song of joy;
and the hope buried in his breast
rang echoing,
from meadow, glade and forest.

Songs of Love

লেখন

স্বপ্ন আমার জোনাকি,
দীপ্ত প্রাণের মণিকা,
স্তব্ধ আঁধার নিশীথে
উড়িছে আলোর কণিকা ॥

My fancies are fireflies
speaks of living light—
twinkling in the dark.

আমার লিখন ফুটে পথধারে
ক্ষণিক কালের ফুলে,
চলিতে চলিতে দেখে যারা তারে
চলিতে চলিতে ভুলে ॥

The same voice murmurs
in these desultory lines
which is born in wayside pansies
letting hasty glances pass by.

প্রজাপতি সেতো বরষ না গণে,
নিমেষ গণিয়া বাঁচে,
সময় তাহার যথেষ্ট তাই আছে ॥

The butterfly does not count years
but moments
and therefore has enough time.

Ei kothaati money rekho, tomaader ei haashi khelaay
aami je gaan geyechhilem,
jeerno paataa jhoraar belaay.
Shukno ghaashey shunyo boney aapon money
onaadorey obohelaay
aami je gaan geyechhilem jeerno paataa jhoraar belaay.
Diner pothik money rekho, aami choleychhilem raatey
Shondhyaaprodeep niye haatey.
Jokhon aamaaye opaar thekey galo dekey
bheshechhilem bhaangaa bhelaay.
Aami je gaan geyechhilem, jeerno paata jhoraar belaay.

Preserve in your memory
in the midst of your joy and laughter
the song I sang in the season
when the leaves were falling.

The grass was withered in the solitary wood
and I alone,
unloved, forsaken;
sang a song in the season
when the leaves were falling.

Remember! Oh traveller of the day,
how I walked into the night
with the evening lamp in my hand.

When the call came for me from a distant shore
I floated away
in my broken bark.
I sang a song in the season
when the leaves were falling.

Aami roopey tomaay bholaabo naa, bhaalobaashaay bholaabo.
Aami haat diye dwaar khulbo naa go, gaan diye dwaar kholaabo.
Bhoraabo naa bhooshon bhaarey, shaajaabonaa phuler haarey—
Premkey aamaar maalaa ko'rey golaay tomaar dolaabo.
Jaanbey naa keu kone tuphaaney torongodol naachbey praaney,
Chaander moton olokh taaney joaarey dheu tolaabo.

I shall lure you not with my beauty
but with my love.
Your door I will open, not with this hand
but with a song.
I shall load you not with precious gems
nor bedeck you with flowers;
my love I shall weave into a garland
and hang it upon your breast.

No one will know what distant storms
make waves within you dance.
Like the straining tide invisible
when the moon is at the full,
I shall make the mighty breakers swell,
like mountains in your soul.

Aamaar jeebon paatro uchholiyaa maadhuri korechho daan—
Tumi jaano naai, tumi jaano naai,
tumi jaano naai, taar mulyer porimaan.
Rojonigondhaa ogochorey
jemon rojoni shwoponey bhorey shourobhey.
Tumi jaano naai, tumi jaano naai,
tumi jaano naai, moromey aamaar dhelechho tomaar gaan.
Bidaay nebaar shomoy ebaar holo—
Proshonno mukh tolo, mukh tolo, mukh tolo—
Modhur moroney poorno koriyaa shonpiyaa jaabo praan choroney.
Jaarey jaano naai, jaarey jaano naai, jaarey jaano naai
Taar gopon byaathaar neerob raatri hoke aaji oboshaan.

You have filled the vessel of my life
with sweetness to the brim
not knowing; never knowing
its immeasurable value.

As the blossoms of the tuberose
fill the night with fragrant dreams,
into the depths of my soul
you have poured your music.

Now that the hour of parting is near
lift up a smiling face, beloved one!
My life enriched with the sweetness of death
shall rest forever at your feet.

Ah! You will never know!
This silent night will see the end
of the secret pain of one
who was ever a stranger to you.

Aaji godhoolilogoney ei baadol gogoney
taar chorondhwoni aami hridoye goni—
'shey aashibey' aamaar mono boley shaaraabelaa,
okaaron pulokey aankhi bhaashey joley.
Odheer poboney taar uttoreeyo doorer poroshon dilo ki o—
Rojonigondhaar porimoley 'shey aashibey' aamaar mono boley.
Utolaa hoyechhey maalotir lotaa,
phuraalonaa taahaar moner kothaa.
Boney boney aaji e ki kaanaakaani,
kisher baarotaa oraa peyechhey naa jaani,
kaanpon laagey digongonaar buker aancholey—
'Shey aashibey' aamaar mono boley.

Clouds hang heavy in the twilit sky.
I count his footsteps in my heart.
An ecstasy unknown dampens my lashes,
as someone within me whispers,
he comes!

His garment streaming in the fevered wind
touches my soul from afar.
In the fragrance of tuberoses white
someone within me whispers,
he comes!

The flowering *malati* sways in anguish
and a murmuring rises in the woodlands;
the veil trembles on the breast of the sky.
Do they too receive the message?
As someone within me whispers,
he comes!

Aami chini go chini tomaarey ogo bideshini.
Tumi thaako shindhupaarey ogo bideshini.
Tomaaye dekhechhi shaarod praatey,
tomaaye dekhechhi maadhobi raatey,
tomaaye dekhechhi hridi-maajhaarey ogo bideshini.
Aami aakaashey paatiya kaan
shunechhi shunechhi tomaari gaan,
aami tomaarey shonpechhi praan ogo bideshini.
Bhubon bhromiyaa sheshey aami eshechhi nooton deshey,
aami otithi tomaari dwaarey ogo bideshini.

I know you lovely alien
I know you!
You live by the shore of a distant ocean
Oh lovely alien!

I have seen you on an autumn morn;
on a flower-scented night.
I have seen you in the closet of my heart.
Oh lovely alien!

Straining my ears to the sky
I have heard snatches of your song
and surrendered my soul to you.

A traveller all over the world
I come to a new country;
at last to your door,
Oh lovely alien!

Aaamaarey koro tomaar beenaa, loho go loho tuley.
Uthibey baaji tontriraaji mohon onguley.
Komole tobo komol korey porosh koro poraan-'porey,
Uthibey hiyaa gunjoriyaa tobo srobonmooley.
Kokhono shukhey kokhono dukhey
kaandibey chaahi tomaar mukhey,
Choroney podi robey nirobey rohibey jobey bhuley.
Keho naa jaaney ki nobo taaney uthibey geet shunyo-paaney,
Aanonder baarotaa jaabey ononter kooley.

Make me your lyre!
Lift me, oh! lift me in your arms.
At the touch of those enchanted fingers
the strings shall burst forth in melody.

Touch my soul
with the tender petals of your lotus hand
and it will murmur
sweet music in your ear.

Sometime in joy, sometime in tears,
it will gaze upon your face;
and when you no more remember,
in silence, lie at your feet.

No one knows what new symphony
will float above to the cosmic spheres,
and what message of joy be transported
to the shores of eternity.

Jhorey jaay urey jaay go aamaar
mukher aancholkhaani.
Dhaakaa thaakey naa haay go,
taarey raakhtey naari taani.
Aamaar shoilo naa laajlojjaa, aamaar ghuchlo go shaajshojjaa–
Tumi dekhley aamaarey emon proloy-maajhey aani
aamaay emon moron haani.
Hothaat aakaash ujoli kaarey khunjey key oi choley,
chomok laagaay bijuli aamaar aandhaar ghorer toley.
Tobey nisheeth gogon jurey, aamaar jaak shokoli urey,
ei daarun kolloley baajuk aamaar praaner baanee
kono baandhon naahi maani.

On this wild night the lashing wind
whips the veil away from my face
leaving it, in spite of all my striving,
exposed to the elements.

I am stripped of all adornment;
no shame nor sorrow is left to me.
You dragged me into this pitiless light
and saw my face,
naked and vulnerable.

Suddenly a flash of lightning illumines the sky
and in the light I see a form,
walking the pathless void
in eternal quest.

Then let the storm rise to a frenzy!
Let all that I call mine
be swept away in a whirl of demoniac fury;
and in the midst of this terrible clamour,
may the words hidden in my heart
well out in a stream of rhapsody—
Ah! blessed, blessed release!

Tumi robey neerobey hridoye momo
nibiro nibhrito poornimaa-nisheethinee shomo.
Momo jeebono joubono momo okhilo bhubono
tumi bhoribey gourobey nisheethinee-shomo.
Jaagibey ekaakee tobo koruno aankhi,
tobo oncholo chaayaa morey rohibey dhaaki.
Momo dukkho bedono momo shopholo shwopono
tumi bhoribey shourobhey nisheethinee-shomo.

You shall dwell in the depths of my heart,
in silence, in secret;
like the radiance of a full moon night.

You shall fill with pride my life, my youth;
my single universe.

Your anguished eyes will wake all night,
gazing fondly on one over whom
you have drawn your mantle with gentle care.

My pain, my anguish, my visions of joy
will be filled with the fragrance
of your tender night.

Megh chhaaye shojol baaye mon aamaar
utolaa korey shaaraabelaa
kaar lupto haashi, shupto bedonaa haaye rey.
Kone boshonter nisheethey jey bokul maalaakhaani poraaley
taar dolguli gachhey jhorey, shudhu gondho bhaashey praaney.
Jaani phiribey naa aar phiribey naa,
jaani poth tobo gachhey shudoorey.
Paariley naa tobu paariley naa
chiroshoonyo koritey bhubon momo–
tumi niye gachho more baanshikhaani, diye gachho tomaar gaan.

When monsoon clouds trail shadows over the earth
driven by a dark wind laden with rain;
whose vanished laughter echoes in my heart?
What dormant pain wells out?
What anguished ecstasy?

On a long forgotten night of spring
you hung on my neck, a garland woven
with soft white stars of dewy *bakul*
whose petals have long since drooped and faded
leaving the fragrance floating upon my soul.

I know your path goes far away
to a point of no return
but you could not, ah! you could not
empty my world and leave me desolate.
You have taken my flute away but left me humming
the last strains of your song.

Aahaa, tomaar shongey praaner khelaa, priyo aamaar, ogo priyo–
Bodo utolaa aaj poraan aamaar, khelaatey haar maanbey ki o.
Kebol tumi-i ki go emni bhaabey raangiye morey paaliye jaabey.
Tumi shaadh korey, naath, dhoraa diye
aamaar o rong bokkhey niyo–
Ei hritkomoler raangaa renu raangaabey oi uttoreeyo.

Ah me! In this game of love with you,
beloved mine, beloved ...
my soul in anguish murmurs,
will you forever win
and I forever lose?

Why is it always you
who takes me unaware?
Come, surrender my Lord with love,
and wear my colour on your breast.

My heart like a new blown lotus,
yields its fragrant pollen ...
living in hope
of staining your garment
in the flames of its crimson hue.

Aamaar kontho hotey gaan key nilo bhulaaye,
shey jey baashaa baandhey neerob moner kulaaye.
Megher diney sraabonmaashey joothiboner deerghoshwaashey
Aamaar praaney shey daay paakhaar chhaayaa bulaaye.
Jokhon shorot kaanpey shiuliphuler horoshey
Noyon bhorey je shei gopon gaaner poroshey.
Gobheer raatey ki shur laagaay aadho-ghumey aadho-jaagaay,
Aamaar shwopon-maajhey daay jey ki dol dulaaye.

Some one has stolen the song from my throat;
she has built a little nest
under the eaves
of my silent soul.

In the season of rain when clouds darken the sky;
when the wild white jasmine wafts a sigh in the air;
she waves over my heart
a gentle rustle
of her shadowy wings.

When tender autumn
shivers with the thrill of her opening buds,
that secret song touches my eyes and makes them weep.
What strains are these
that in the dark of night
ring in my dreams and make me sway,
half in wakefulness
and half in sleep?

Hey kkhoniker otithi,
Eley probhaatey kaarey chaahiyaa
jhoraa sheyphaalir potho baahiyaa.
Kone omoraar birohineerey chaaho ni phirey,
kaar bishaader shishiro neerey eley naahiyaa.
Ogo okorun, ki maayaa jaano,
Milon chholey biroho aano.
Choleychho pothik aalokojaaney aandhaar-paaney
Monbhulaano mohon taaney gaan gaahiyaa.

Seeking whom did you come with the early dawn,
treading softly on a path
strewn with *shiuli* blooms;
guest of a moment?

What immortal lover is from you estranged?
Why bathed in drops of anguished dew,
you pass on in silence, with never a glance behind?

Ah! ruthless one! What spell is yours
that brings pain and parting
in the guise of happy union?

Walking on the path of light, towards a nameless dark,
you sing a song with strains serene,
enthralling mind and soul.

Aashaa jaaoaar pother dhaarey gaan geye more ketechhey din.
Jaabaar belaay debo kaarey buker kaachhey baajlo jey been.
Shurguli taar naanaa bhaagey rekhey jaabo pushpo raagey;
meedguli taar megher rekhaay shwornolekhaay korbo bileen.
Kichhu baa shey milon maalaay jugol golaay roibey gaanthaa,
kichhu baa shey bhijiye debey dui chaahonir chokher paataa.
Kichhu baa kone choitromaashey bokul-dhaakaa boner ghaashey
moner kothaar tukro aamaar kuriye paabey kone udaasheen.

I have spent my days singing by the path
where life moves to and fro.
To whom shall I leave, now my hour is near,
this lyre that plays in my soul?

Fragments of song will flash from the facets
of priceless gems of old;
the cadence will merge in the edges of clouds
in etchings of gleaming gold.

A strain or two may be strung in the wreaths
that on breasts of lovers dance;
and another will sparkle in the melting drops,
shadowing a mutual glance.

And in fragrant March when the grass in the wood
is covered with *bakul* flowers,
a wandering minstrel perchance may find
the remnant of a word.

Aamaar jaabaar belaay pichhu daakey
bhorer aalo megher phaankey phaankey.
Baadol praater udaash paakhi othey daaki
boner gopon shaakhey shaakhey, pichhu daakey.
Bhoraa nodi chhaayaar toley chhutey choley–
Khonjey kaakey, pichhu daakey.
Aamaar praaner bhitor shey key thekey thekey
bidaay praater utolaakey pichhu daakey.

Now that the hour of parting is near,
I hear a call,
in the light of the dawn; through crevices of clouds.

A wild bird's cry breaks the grey lull
of a sky overcast with cloud;
from her secret nest, among the boughs
I hear her call.

The flooded river goes rushing by
through shadows of winding trees.
For whom this ceaseless, anguished search?
For whom this frenzied cry?

Within my heart, in a whispering voice
on this bleak farewell morn;
again and again, in broken words
I hear a call.

Dinaantobelaay sheysher phoshol nilem tori-'porey,
e paarey krishi holo shaaraa,
Jaabo opaarer ghaatey.
Hongsho bolaakaa udey jaay, durer teerey, taaraar aaloye,
taari daanaar dhwoni baajey more ontorey.
Bhaantaar nodi dhaay shaagor paaney kolotaaney,
Bhaabona more bheshey jaay taari taaney.
Jaa-kichhu niye choli shesh shonchoy
Shukh noy shey, dukkho shey noy, noy shey kaamonaa
Shuni shudhu maajhir gaan aar daanrer dhwoni taahaar shworey.

At wane of day I fill my bark
with the last fruits of my toil.
My work is done; my time has come
to sail to the distant bank...

where fly a stream of stately swans
in the light of the evening star;
and the beat of their wings in the gathering dusk
makes music in my heart.

The river rushes to the sea
in a wild rhapsody—
drawing my thoughts on the ebb of tide
like a pensive symphony.

I take with me all that is mine
not joy, not pain, not yearning;
only the echoes of the boatman's song
and the plash of his oars in the gloaming.

Tomaarei koriyaachhi jeeboner dhrubotaaraa,
e shomudrey aar kobhu hobo naako potho haaraa.
Jethaa aami jaayi naako tumi prokaashito thaako,
aakul noyonjoley dhaalo go kirondhaaraa.
Tobo mukh shodaa money jaagitechhey shongoponey,
Tilek ontor holey naa heri kool-kinaaraa.
Kokhono bipothey jodi bhromitey chaahey e hridi
Omni o mukh heri shoromey shey hoy shaaraa.

I have made you my lodestar;
I shall follow your light.
Never again shall I flounder
in this ocean of life.

I sense your presence wherever I roam.
The rays from your tender eyes
fall on my copious tears in streams
of irridiscent light.

Your face appears in secret stealth
in the mirror of my heart.
And if, perchance, it floats away
I grope blindly in the dark.

And when this self is led astray
from the path that it must take,
you show your face; I hang my head,
consumed with guilt and shame.

Ekhono taarey chokhey dekhini, shudhu baanshi shunechhi—
Mon praan jaahaa chhilo diye pheleychhi.
Shunechhi muroti kaalo taarey naa dekhaa bhaalo.
Shokhi, bolo aami jol aanitey jomunaaye jaabo ki.
Shudhu shwoponey esheychhilo shey,
noyon koney hesheychhilo shey
Shey obodhi, shoi, bhoye bhoye roi—
aankhi melitey bhebey shaaraa hoi.
Kaanonpothey jey khushi shey jaaye,
kodom toley jey khushi shey chaaye—
Shokhi, bolo aami aankhi tuley kaaro paaney chaabo ki.

I have not seen him yet.
I have only heard his flute,
yet all I had of heart and soul
to him I have given
in sweet surrender.

I'm told so dark is he,
his form is better not to see.
Should I to the river go, dear friend,
my water pot to fill?

He came only in my dreams—
eyes smiling tenderly;
since then I'm all a-tremble,
shy of lifting my lashes.

Whoever wishes may walk in the gardens,
may gaze upon the shadows in the *kadamba* grove;
but tell me dear friend,
dare I raise my eyes
and look on him?

Baajilo kaahaar beenaa modhur shworey
Aamaar nibhrito nobo jeebon- 'porey.
Probhaat komolo shomo phutilo hridoy momo
Kaar duti nirupom choron-torey.
Jegey uthey shob shobhaa, shob maadhuri,
Polokey polokey hiyaa pulokey poori.
Kothaa hotey shomeeron aaney nobo jaagoron,
poraaner aaboron mochon korey.
Laagey bukey shukhey dukhey koto jey byaathaa,
Kamoney bujhaaye kobo naa jaani kothaa.
Aamaaro baashonaa aaji tribhuboney uthey baaji,
kaanpey nodi bonoraaji bedonaabhorey.

I know not whose lyre
plays a sweet symphony
in this secret dawn of my life;
my heart like a lotus in the morn
opens its thousand petals
beneath those peerless feet.

To the strains of that music,
beauty awakes;
her heart filling with bliss
from moment to moment.

From where do the winds of spring
bring this awakening,
rending the veils of the soul?

I find no words to describe
this painful strife
of agony and joy in my breast!

My desire rings echoing
through the three worlds,
and the river and the woodlands
tremble with the poignancy of my pain.

Jodi jaantem aamaar kisher byaathaa tomaaye jaanaataam.
Key jey aamaay kaandaay aami ki jaani taar naam.
Kothaay jey haat baadaai michhey, phiri aami kaahaar pichhey—
Shob jano more bikiyechhey, paaini taahaar daam.
Ei bedonaar dhon shey kothaay bhaabi jonom dhorey.
Bhubon bhorey aachhey jano, paaini jeebon bhorey.
Shukh jaarey koy shokol joney baajaai taarey khoney khoney—
Gobheer shurey 'chaainey' 'chaainey' baajey obisraam.

If I knew the cause of my pain
I would tell it to you, my friend;
someone makes me weep
but do I know his name?

I know not where I stretch my arms,
whom I pursue in vain,
It seems to me that I have sold
my all, for no exchange.

Through my life I've asked, *Where lies*
this priceless gem of pain?
Wasting my life in futile search,
though it fills the universe.

All day I play on the strings of my lyre
of joy as humans know,
but *no, not for me!* the sombre tones
echo endless in my soul.

Olo shoi, olo shoi, aamaar ichhey korey toder moton
moner kothaa koi.
Chodiye diye paa dukhaani koney boshey kaanaakaani,
kobhu heshey kobhu kendey cheye boshey roi.
Olo shoi, olo shoi,
toder aachhey moner kothaa, aamaar aachhey koi.
Aami ki bolibo, kaar kothaa, kone shukh, kone byaathaa—
Naai kothaa tobu shaadh shoto kothaa koi.
Olo shoi, olo shoi,
Toder eto ki bolibaar aachhey bhebey obaak hoi.
Aami ekaa boshi shondhyaa holey
aapni bhaashi noyonjoley,
kaaron keho shudhaailey neerob hoye roi.

Friend, dear friend!
I wish I could pour out like you
the thoughts that vex my soul ...
legs stretched out in a corner;
now laughing, now weeping,
now staring at the floor.

Friend, dear friend!
Streams of words flow from your lips.
Why am I so bereft?
What can I share? With whom and when?
What pain? What joy? What inmost hopes?
I long to speak as you do, friend
but no words come to me.

Friend, dear friend!
So much there is that you speak of.
Where lies the source I wonder!
I sit alone as dusk descends
wallowing in my tears.
And if one asks wherefore I weep
I have no answer why.

Hey shokhaa, baarotaa peyechhi money money
tobo nishwaashporoshoney,
Esheychho odekhaa bondhu dokkhinshomeeroney.
Kano bonchonaa koro morey, kano baandho odrishyo dorey—
Dekhaa daao, dekhaa daao deho mon bho'rey
momo nikunjoboney.
Dekhaa daao chompokey rongoney,
dekhaa daao kinshukey kaanchoney.
Kano shudhu baanshorir shurey bhulaaye loye jaao doorey,
joubon-utshobey dhoraa daao drishtir bondhoney.

I have felt your message within my heart
with the touch of your breath, my friend;
you are come, oh! invisible one
on the sweet winds of the south.

Why am I tied with unseen bonds;
eyes robbed of your fair form?
Reveal yourself in my lonely bower
filling body, mind and soul.

Reveal yourself in the purple and gold
of the *kanchan* and *champak* flower;
in the ixora's ruby and the forest flame's
blaze of crimson fire.

Why does your flute lure me far away
making waves within me dance?
In this festival of youth, come surrender
to the bonds of a mutual glance.

Tobu money rekho jodi doorey jaai choley.
Jodi puraaton prem dhaakaa porey jaay nobopremjaaley.
Jodi thaaki kaachhaakaachhi,
dekhitey naa paao chhaayaar moton aachhi naa aachhi—
tobu money rekho.
Jodi jol aashey aankhipaatey,
ek din jodi khelaa themey jaay modhuraatey,
tobu money rekho.
Ek din jodi baadhaa porey kaajey shaarod praatey—money rekho.
Jodi poriyaa money
Chholochholo jol naai dekhaa daay noyonokoney—
tobu money rekho.

Remember me
if ever I go far far away;
if old love gets trapped and hidden
in a web of new desire;
if by your side I be
close like a shadow which you cannot see,
remember me.

If ever tears well up in the corners of your eyes;
if all games end on a secret, honeyed night;
remember me.

If on an autumn morn something
stops you in your task;
if remembering, no pearl drops of tears
gleam on dark lashes;
still remember me.

Songs of the Motherland

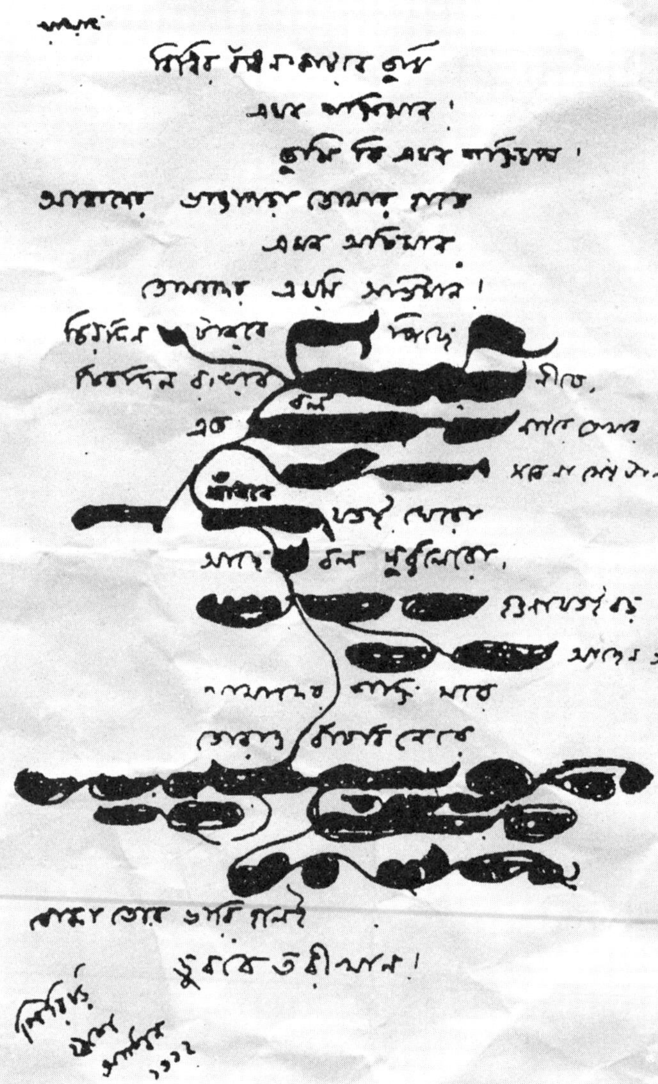

নিবিড় সঘন অন্ধকারে তুমি
এমন অভিসার!
তুমি কি এমন অভিসার!
আকাশের অন্তরালে তোমার যাত্রা
এমন অভিসার
তোমাদের এমনি অভিসার!
চিরদিন [redacted] তোমারে [redacted] নিতে [redacted]
চিরদিন [redacted] নীচে,
এত [redacted] মনে মনে
[redacted] মনে মনে দেখা দিল!
[redacted] যত যেতে
আজি [redacted] জল দুলিছে,
[redacted] ঢেকেছে রে
[redacted] আলো
[redacted] বাদল মাঝে
তোমার সোনার বেশে
[redacted]
কাহার তোমার ভালো গানে
দুর্বলে তরী খান!

Jonogonomono odhinaayok joyo hey
Bhaarot bhaagyo bidhaataa

Punjaab Shindhu Gujaraat Maraathaa
Draabid Utkol Bongo
Bindhyo Himaachol Jomunaa Gongaa
uchholo jolodhi torongo
Tobo shubho naamey jaagey,
tobo shubho aashish maagey,
gaahey tobo joyogaathaa.
Jonogonomongol daayok joyo hey
Bhaarot bhaagyo bidhaataa
joyo hey, joyo hey, joyo hey
joyo joyo joyo, joyo hey.

Ohoroho tobo aaobhaan prochaarito,
shuni tobo udaar baanee
Hindu Bauddho Shikh Joino Paaroshik
Musholmaan Khrishtaani
Purob Poshchim aashey tobo sinhaashon paashey
premhaar hoy gaanthaa.
Jonogono-oikyo bidhaayok joyo hey
bhaarot bhaagyo bidhaataa
joyo hey, joyo hey, joyo hey
joyo joyo joyo, joyo hey.

Leader of the masses.
Lord of the minds of men.
Arbiter of India's destiny.
Hail to you! All hail!

Your name resounds through her sea and land
waking countless sleeping souls
from Punjab, Sindh, Gurarat, Maratha
to Dravid, Utkal, Banga.
Her mighty mountains—Himachal, Vindhya,
her rivers—Yamuna, Ganga,
the blue green sea with which she is girdled;
her waves, her peaks, her rippling air
seek your blessing, carry your echoes.
Oh boundless good! Oh merciful!
Hail to you! All hail!

At the sound of your call the people assemble
from myriad streams of life.
Hindu, Muslim, Buddhist, Jain.
Christian, Parsee and Sikh.
East and West stand by your throne
hands held in amity,
weaving a wreath of fraternal love;
of empathy, unity.
Oh you who bring us all together!
Hail to you! All hail!

Potono-obhyudoyo-bondhur ponthaa
jug jug dhaabito jaatri.
Hey chiroshaarothi, tobo rothochokrey
mukhorito poth din raatri.
Daaroon biplobo-maajhey tobo shonkhodhwoni baajey
shonkoto dukkho traata.
Jonogono poth porichaayok joyo hey
Bhaarot bhaagyo bidhaataa
joyo hey, joyo hey, joyo hey
joyo joyo joyo, joyo hey.

Ghor timirghono nibiro nisheethey
peerito moorchhito deshey
jaagroto chhilo tobo obichol mongol notonoyoney onimeshey.
Dushwopney aatonkey rokkhaa koriley onkey
snehomoyee tumi maataa.
Jonogonodukkho traayok joyo hey
Bhaarot bhaagyo bidhaataa
joyo hey, joyo hey, joyo hey,
joyo joyo joyo, joyo hey.

Raatri probhaatilo, udilo robichhobi
poorbo-udoygiribhaaley—
Gaahey bihongom, punyo shomeeron
nobojeebonrosho dhaaley.
Tobo korunaarun raagey nidrito Bhaarot jaagey
tobo choroney noto maathaa.
Joyo joyo joyo hey, joyo raajeshwor
Bhaarot bhaagyo bidhaataa
Joyo hey, joyo hey, joyo hey,
joyo joyo joyo, joyo hey

Nations rise and nations fall
on the perilous path of history.
And you Eternal Charioteer
guide the world's destiny.
Through day, through night, your wheels are heard
renting the air with sound,
dispelling terror, banishing pain;
blowing the conch of peace.
Oh true arbiter of India's fate!
Hail to you! All hail!

In the deep dark of a turbulent night,
when our swooning, suffering land
lifted her eyes to your face in hope,
she saw your unwavering gaze
raining blessings, alight with love,
banishing evil dreams.
Like a loving mother you held out your arms
and changed her destiny.
Oh you who wipe out the pain of the masses!
Hail to you! All hail!

A new day dawns; a new sun rises
from the mountains of the east.
Song birds trill; new sap of life
is borne on the holy breeze.
India awakes from aeons of slumber
to the strains of your lofty song.
Head bowed to your feet oh King of kings!
Hail to you! All hail!

Orey, nooton juger bhorey
dish ney shomoy kaatiye brithaa shomoy bichaar korey.
Ki robey aar ki robey naa, ki hobey aar ki hobey naa orey hishaabi,
e shongshoyer maajhey ki tor bhaabnaa mishaabi?
Jamon korey jhornaa naamey durgom porbotey
Nirbhaabnaay jhaanp diye por ojaaniter pothey.
Jaagbey totoi shokti jotoi haanbey torey maanaa,
Ojaanaakey bosh korey tui korbi aapon jaanaa.
Cholaay cholaay baajbey joyer bheree—
Paayer begeyi poth ketey jaay, korish ney aar deri.

A new day dawns.
Waste not your time in empty speculation.
What is, what is not, what will, what will not.
Blend not your fears with this your hesitation.
A new day dawns ...

As the mountain torrent gushes tempestuous down
innumerable chasms, strange untrodden paths;
do you oh fearless, leap with a lusty spring
into this brave new world; a vast unknown.

Perilous peaks of resistance lying across your path;
with ever soaring strength shall you subdue.
Vaulting, reckless, into uncharted land;
taming and conquering the vast unknown.

With feet of glory you shall cut out your path.
The roll of drums announce your triumphal march;
delay not, a new day dawns.

Oder baandhon jotoi shokto hobey totoi baandhon tutbey,
moder totoi baandhon tutbey.
Oder jotoi aankhi rokto hobey moder aankhi phutbey,
totoi moder aankhi phutbey.
Aaaj key jey tor kaaj koraa chaai,
shwopno dekhaar shomoy to naai—
Ekhon oraa jotoi gorjaabey, bhaai, tondraa totoi chhutbey,
moder tondraa totoi chhutbey.
Oraa bhaangtey jotoi chaa'bey jorey gorbey totoi dwigun korey,
oraa jotoi raagey maarbey rey ghaa totoi jey dheu uthbey.
Toraa bhorshaa naa chharish kobhu, jegey aachhen jogot-probhu—
Oraa dhormo jotoi dolbey totoi dhoolaay dhwojaa lutbey,
oder dhoolaay dhwojaa lutbey.

The tighter they tie our limbs,
the sooner our bonds will break.
The harsher the glare of their bloodshot eyes
the clearer our eyes shall see.

Now is the hour for ceaseless work;
no time for empty dreams.
The louder they roar, the sooner oh! brothers,
our slumber shall shattered be.

The harder they try to break with force
the stronger shall they build.
The more they strike with frenzied hate,
wave upon wave will spring.

Lose not hope you suffering souls.
The Lord of the Earth still wakes.
If they trample the truth beneath their heels
their flag will be dragged in the dust;
their proud flag will be dragged in the dust.

Shonkocher bihbholotaa nijeyrey opomaan,
shonkoter kolponaatey hoyonaa mriyomaan!
Mukto koro bhoy, aaponaa maajhey shokti dhoro, nijeyrey koro joy.
Durboleyrey rokkha koro, durjoneyrey haano,
nijeyrey deen nihshohaay jano kobhu naa jaano.
Mukto koro bhoy, nijer porey koritey bhor naa rekho shongshoy.
Dhormo jobey, shonkhorobey, koribey aaobhaan
neerob hoye, nomro hoye, pon koriyo praan.
Mukto koro bhoy, duruho kaajey nijeyrey diyo kothin porichoy.

Turn not bewilderment into a source of humiliation.
Let not imagined perils make you lose your track.
Cast out fear!
Be strong and conquer self.

Think not of yourself as small and helpless.
Protect the weak; strike at the wicked.
Cast out fear!
Control your destiny.

When truth commands to the sound of blowing conches;
in meek silence set your soul at stake.
Cast out fear!
Attain the unattainable.

Jodi tor daak shuney keu naa aashey tobey eklaa cholo rey.
eklaa cholo, eklaa cholo, eklaa cholo, eklaa cholo rey.
Jodi keu kothaa naa koy, orey orey o obhaagaa,
jodi shobaai thaakey mukh phiraaye shobaai korey bhoy—
Tobey poraan khuley
o tui mukh phutey tor moner kothaa eklaa bolo rey.
Jodi shobaai phirey jaay, orey orey o obhaagaa
jodi gohon pothey jaabaar kaaley keu phirey naa chaay—
Tobey pother kaantaa
o tui roktomaakhaa chorontoley eklaa dolo rey.
Jodi aalo naa dhorey, orey orey o obhaagaa,
jodi jhor-baadoley aandhaar raatey dooar daye ghorey—
Tobey bojraanoley
aapon buker paanjor jwaaliye niye eklaa jwolo rey.

If no one answers to your call
go your way alone.

If all are mute, oh! hapless one,
if all are filled with fear,
then open your heart in a fearless burst
and speak the truth alone.

If all go back, oh! hapless one,
when you are on your way
along the deep, dark forest track,
if no one turns his face;
then walk the thorny path
on proudly bleeding feet,
with face set bravely forward,
the bloodstained dust behind.

If no one lights the beacon
on a dark and stormy night;
if no one hears your knocking
and all men shut their doors;
then lose not heart oh! hapless one
but in the fiery thunder
set the torch of your heart aflame
and burn in the dark alone.

Aamraa mileychhi aaj maayer daakey.
Ghorer hoye porer moton bhaai chherey bhaai kodin thaakey?
Praaner maajhey thekey thekey 'aay' boley oi dekechhey key,
shei gobheer shworey udaash korey—aar key kaarey dhorey raakhey?
Jethaay thaaki jey jeykhaaney baandhon aachhey praaney praaney,
shei praaner taaney teney aaney—
shei praaner bedon jaaney naa key?
Maan opomaan gachhey ghuchey, noyoner jol gachhey muchhey—
shei nobeen aashey hridoy bhaashey bhaaier paashey bhaaikey dekhey.
Koto diner shaadhonpholey milechhi aaj doley doley—
aaj ghorer chheley shobaai miley dekhaa diye aay rey maakey.

We're here together at our Mother's call
Come, come my children ...
Can brothers remain as if they were strangers
when the voice of the Mother is heard in the heart?

Scattered though we are in our own little worlds
our lives are tied with a single cord
which pulls us together despite all distance
in mutual agony; a common bond.

We have wiped our tears away for ever,
deemed humiliation a thing of the past;
a new hope fills our swelling breasts,
seeing brother stand by brother's side.

Aeons have passed in patient striving
and today we assemble in masses.
Come let us join hands oh! sons of the land
and shout back in answer, *We come!*

Bidhir baandhon kaatbey tumi emon shoktimaan—
tumi ki emni shoktimaan!
Aamaader bhaangaa goraa tomaar haatey emon obhimaan—
tomaader emni obhimaan.
Chirodin taanbey pichhey, chirodin raakhbey neechey—
eto bol naai rey tomaar, shobey naa shei taan.
Shaashoney jotoi ghero aachhey bol durbolero,
ho o naa jotoi boro aachhen bhogobaan.
Aamaader shokti merey toraa o baanchbi ney rey
bojhaa tor bhaari holei dubbey torikhaan.

Do you believe you have the power
to burst the bonds of fate?
Ah! Vain boast,
to think that we are in your hands
to make or break at will.

Can you pull us back forever
ground in the dust beneath your heel?
With a mighty twang the rope will snap
proving your vaunt was all in vain.

Inflict your rule with ruthless hate;
the weak can yet be strong.
Though you be great, there is one greater;
He is Almighty God.

If you crush the strength from our feeble limbs
yours will surely fail;
when the load of your guilt grows heavy
your boat will totter and sink
in the ocean of the Omnipotent.

O aamaar desher maati, tomaar porey thekaai maathaa.
Tomaatey bishwomoyeer, tomaatey bishwo maayer aanchol paataa.
Tumi misheychho more deher shoney,
tumi milechho more praaney money,
tomaar oi shyaamol boron komole moorti mormey gaanthaa.
Ogo maa, tomaar koley jonom aamaar moron tomaar bukey.
Tomaar porey khelaa aamaar dukkhey shukhey.
Tumi onno mukhey tuley diley,
tumi sheetol joley juraailey,
tumi jey shokol-shohaa shokol-bohaa maataar maataa.
O maa, onek tomaar kheyechhi go, onek niyechhi maa—
tobu jaani ney jey ki baa tomaay diyechhi maa!
Aamaar jonom galo brithaa kaajey,
aami kaataanu din ghorer maajhey—
tumi brithaa aamaay shokti diley shoktidaataa.

Ah! the soil of my country!
I bow my head to you;
for over you the earth,
your mighty mother, has spread her veil
in gentle protective care.

You are mingled with my life and soul
you are merged within my body;
the image of your darksome beauty
is welded in the sources of my being.
I was born in your lap, oh my mother.
May I die upon your breast!

I have run to your bosom
in joy and in sorrow,
you have fed me and bathed me
in your cool green waters;
you who can bear all burdens, suffer all anguish,
for your children, oh mother of mothers!

I have taken my all from you,
given nothing in return ...
I have hidden myself in the confines of my chamber
and wasted my life in vain pursuits.
Ah! where has it gone, dispenser of power,
the power I received from you?

Nishidin bhorshaa raakhish, orey mon, hobei hobey.
Jodi pon korey thaakish shey pon tomaar robei robey.
Orey mon, hobei hobey.
Paashaan shomaan aachhey porey, praan peye shey uthbey orey,
aachhey jaaraa bobaar moton taaraao kothaa kobei kobey.
Shomoy holo, shomoy holo—jey jaar aapon bojhaa tolo rey—
Dukkho jodi maathaay dhorish shey dukkho tor shobei shobey.
Ghontaa jokhon uthbey bejey dekhbi shobaai aashbey shejey—
Ek shaathey shob jaatri joto ek i raastaa lobei lobey.

Night and day keep faith, my soul;
what you desire shall be.
If you have sworn an oath,
your word shall honoured be.

The mountain lying in your path
shall stir with a waking soul.
From tongues that are mute today
words will surely flow.

The hour is near, the hour is near!
Lift up your burdens, all.
If sorrow you bear with courage
in readiness for the call ...

then, when the gong starts striking,
ah! what a wondrous sight.
Pilgrims walking your chosen path
in thousands by your side.

Chhi chhi, chokher joley bhejaash ney aar maati.
Ebaar kothin hoye thaak naa orey, bokkho dooar aanti—
jorey bokkho dooar aanti.
Poraantaakey goliye pheley dish ney, rey bhaai, pothey dheley
mithyey okaajey—
Orey niye taarey cholbi paarey kotoi baadhaa kaati,
pother kotoi baadhaa kaati.
Dekhley o tor joler dhaaraa ghorey porey haashbey jaaraa
taaraa chaar dikey—
Taader dwaarei giye kaanna jurish, jaaye naa ki buk phaati,
laajey jaaye naa ki buk phaati?
Diner belaa jogot-maajhey shobaai jokhon cholchhey kaajey
aapon gorobey—
toraa pother dhaarey byaathaa niye korish ghaantaa-ghaanti
kebol korish ghaantaa-ghaanti.

For shame!
Let not your tears fall on the ground unheeded.
Lock the gates of your heart.
Lock the gates of your heart with bars of steel.

Pour not your melting soul in useless tasks
along the weary road.
Carry it across to the other bank
braving perilous hazards;
braving perilous hazards on the way.

Surrounding you on every side
are men who mock your streaming tears.
Yet at their doors you weep and wail.
Does not your heart burst?
Does not your heart burst with shame?

In the light of day when over the world
all march to work in pride and hope,
you are seen sitting by the path
playing with your pain;
playing with your pain in idleness.

Jey torey paagol boley taarey tui bolish ney kichhu.
Aajkey torey kamon bhebey ongey jey tor dhulo debey
kaal shey praatey maalaa haatey aashbey rey tor pichhu pichhu.
Aajkey aapon maaner bhorey thaak shey boshey godir' porey—
kaalkey premey aashbey nemey, korbey shey taar maathaa neechu.

They call you mad! Do not heed them.
Those that throw dust on you today
shall come with garlands of sweet scented flowers
and follow you from morn till night,
on the morrow.

It matters not that vain and proud
they sit today on pompous thrones.
They must climb down with heads hung low
and come to you with love,
on the morrow.

Aami bhoy korbo naa bhoy korbo naa.
Du belaa moraar aagey morbo naa, bhaai morbo naa.
Torikhaanaa baaitey geley maajhey maajhey tuphaan meley—
taai boley haal chherey diye dhorbo naa, kaannaakaati dhorbo naa.
Shokto jaa taai shaadhtey hobey, maathaa tuley roibo bhobey—
shohoj pothey cholbo bhebey porbo naa, paanker 'porey porbo naa.
Dhormo aamaar maathaay rekhey cholbo shidhey raastaa dekhey—
bipod jodi eshey porey shorbo naa, ghorer koney shorbo naa.

I shall not die before my death
I shall know no fear.
If my bark is knocked by a tempest
in the heart of the swelling deep,
I shall not drop the oars, oh brothers!
Nor hold my head and weep.

I must pursue the difficult
and keep my head held high.
In walking the easy path I'll surely fall
into the slough and die.

I shall march bravely forth
trust in my destiny;
meet with scorn all perils
on the road to victory.

শুধায়ো না, কবে কোন্ গান
কাহারে করিয়াছিনু দান।
পথের ধুলার 'পরে
পড়ে আছে তারি তরে
যে তাহারে দিতে পারে মান।

তুমি কি শুনেছ মোর বাণী,
হৃদয়ে নিয়েছ তারে টানি'?
জানি না তোমার নাম,
তোমারেই সঁপিলাম
আমার ধ্যানের ধনখানি ॥

[illegible]

Songs of the Seasons

①
= 90
6
8
EK TU KU CHO YA LA- GE - - - E K TU KU KA THA SU NE - - -
TA IE DE YA MO-NE MO NE- - - - - RA CHI MAMO FA- - - L GU NE -
KE-CHU PA LA SHAR NE SHA- - - KE-CHU BACH PAYA MAY SHA - -
TA I DE YA SU RE SU - RE - - - - RAN GA R SE JA L BU NE - -

Poorno chaander maayaay aaji bhaabnaa aamaar poth bholey,
Jano shindhupaarer paakhi taaraa, jaaye jaaye jaaye choley.
Aalochhaayaar shurey onek kaaler shey kone doorey
daakey aaye aaye aaye bo'ley.
Jethaaye choley gachhey aamaar haaraa phaagunraati
shethaaye taaraa phirey phirey khonjey aapon shaathi.
Aalochhaayaay jethaa onek diner shey kone byaathaa
kaandey haay haay haay bo'ley.

On this charmed night when the moon is full
my thoughts lose trail like a stream of birds
that from across a distant ocean,
fly far, far, far away.

To the haunting melody of light and shade
they call from beyond both time and space—
Come, come, come away ...

Beating their wings in an alien sky,
each one his mate, they search;
there, where I lost, long long ago,
my night of fragrant March.

There where buried in light and shade,
a timeless anguish dwells and weeps—
Ah me! ah me! ah me!

Shushko taaper doittyopurey dwaar bhaangbey boley,
raajputro, kothaa hotey hothaat eley choley.
Shaat shomudro-paarer thekey bojro shworey eley henkey,
dundubhi jey uthlo bejey bishom koloroley.
Beerer podoporosh peye moorchhaa hotey jaagey,
boshundhoraar topto praaney bipul pulok laagey.
Morokot monir thaalaa shaajiye gaanthey boronmaalaa,
Utolaa taar hiyaa aaji shojol haaoaaye doley.

To crash the mighty gates, in the land of the demons
of pitiless thirst and fiercely raging heat;
brave prince, from where did you appear
sudden upon this shimmering horizon?

Perchance from the land of the seven seas,
echoing thunder in your mighty voice,
the dark sky rent in terrible commotion
from the deafening roll of your drums of war.

At the touch of a valiant warrior's foot
the fainting earth revives;
and her heart, all fire and dust,
thrills with a tremor fine.

She weaves a garland of welcome
of priceless emeralds;
green as her heart when swayed with a breath
of fragrant rain-drenched air.

Esho shyaamol shundor,
aano tobo taapohoraa trishaahoraa shongoshudhaa.
Birohinee chaahiyaa aachhey aakaashey.
Shey jey byaathito hridoy aachhey bichhaaye
tomaal kunjopothey shojol chaayaatey,
noyoney jaagichhey korun raaginee.
Bokul mukul rekhechhey gaanthiyaa,
baajichhey ongoney milon baanshori.
Aano shaathey tomaar mondiraa
chonchol nrittyer baajibey chhondey shey—
baajibey konkono baajibey kinkinee,
jhonkaaribey monjeer runu runu.

Come, dark beauteous one!
Bring with you the ambrosial stream
of your cooling, quenching presence.
A forsaken woman gazes on the sky in hope.

She has spread her anguished heart
along the shades of the *tamaal* grove.
In her moist eyes awaken
a symphony of sorrow.

She has woven a welcome garland
of scented *bakul* blossoms.
Somewhere a flute is playing
a tune of reunion.

Bring with you your cymbals;
clashing them in rhythm
to a restless dance.
To the tinkling of bracelets,
the jingling of girdles
and the wild jangle
of gleaming gold anklets.

Neelaanjono chhaayaa, prophullo kodombobono,
jombupunjey shyaam bonaanto, bonobithikaa ghono shugondho.
Monthor nobo neeloneerodo porikeerno digonto.
Chitto more ponthohaaraa kaanto birohokaantaarey.

Blue-eyed shadows, flowering *kadamba* groves.
Rose-apple sprays on green forest fringes.
Delicious odours melting in vapours
through tree-lined vistas ... to the darkening sky.

Jewel-blue clouds, new-risen, lush, languorous
sweeping horizons,
and my lovelorn soul like a lost traveller
seeks a path forgotten—
a woman parted in pain from her loveless lover.

Timir-obogunthoney bodon tobo dhaaki
key tumi momo ongoney daanraaley ekaaki.
Aaji shoghono shorboree, meghomogon taaraa,
nodir joley jhorjhori jhorichhey jolodhaaraa,
tomaalbon mormori pobon choley haanki.
Jey kothaa momo ontorey aanichho tumi taani
jaani naa kone montorey taahaarey dibo baanee.
Royechhi baandhaa bondhoney, chhinribo, jaabo baatey—
jano e brithaa krondoney e nishi naahi kaatey.
Kothin baadhaa-longhoney dibo naa aami phaanki.

Veiling your face in the darkness of night,
who are you
standing solitary on my threshold?

Tonight the sky is dark and deep;
the stars are lost in the thickening clouds.
Rain pelts into the river in unceasing torrents
and a wild wind shrieks in the *tamaal* grove

The thought that you have planted in my soul
struggles to find expression.
Oh! where can I find the charm
which will loosen my mute tongue
and make it speak?

I shall tear the bonds stifling me,
shatter all barriers;
release myself upon the path
and waste not the night in bitter tears.

Mon more megher shongee,
urey choley dig digonter paaney
nihsheem shunye sraabon borshon shongeetey
rimijhim rimijhim rimijhim.
Mon more hongsho bolaakaar paakhaay jaay urey
Kkochit kkochit chokit torit-aalokey.
Jhon-jhon monjeer baajaay jhonjhaa rudro aanondey.
kolo-kolo kolomondrey nirjhorinee
daak daay proloy-aaobhaaney.
Baayu bohey poorbo shomudro hotey
uchholo chholo-chholo totinee torongey.
Mon more dhaay taari motto probaahey taal-tomaal-oronye
kkhubdho shaakhaar aandoloney.

A cloud's companion, my mind flies away
beyond the distant horizon, into the endless void,
to the splashing rhythm of a song of the rain.

My mind flies away on the wings of a swan,
that rushes through the sky
amid flashes of lightning;
the clash of cymbals—angry thunder,
and the gurgling joy of the falling rain.

A great cry rises from the depths of the sky;
a call of welcome, for the mighty storm.

Strong gusts rise from the dancing waves
frothing the shores of the eastern sea.
In quest of that surge my heart races in joy
through groves of palms swaying in dance,
the angry movement of lashing fronds.

Chhaayaa ghonaaichhey boney boney,
gogoney gogoney daakey deyaa.
Kobey noboghono-borishoney goponey goponey eli keyaa.
Poorobey neerob ishaaraatey ekodaa nidraaheen raatey
haaoaatey ki pothey dili kheyaa—
aashaarher kheyaaler kone kheyaa.
Jey modhu hridoye chhilo maakhaa
kaantaatey ki bhoye dili dhaakaa.
Bujhi eli jaar obhishaarey money money dekhaa holo taarey,
aarhaaley aarhaaley deyaa-neyaa—
aaponaay lukaaye deyaa-neyaa.

Shadows deepen in the woods;
cloud-calls echo from sky to sky.

Ah! *keya*
On an eve, shadowy with new falling rain,
you came in secret.

On a night of wakeful anguish,
when the east beckoned in silence,
in wild caprice on a pathless monsoon wind
you set your bark afloat.

The honey that filled your heart you hid,
with prickly thorns from fear:

Maybe he, with whom you had a tryst
has come to you in silence,
in the secret recesses of your soul;
and concealing yourselves in the shadows,
you have given and received
in mutual ecstasy.

Baadol meghey maadol baajey guru guru gogon-maajhey.
Taari gobheer roley aamaar hridoy doley,
aapon shurey aapni bholey.
Kothaay chhilo gohono praaney gopon byaathaa gopon gaaney—
Aaji shojol baaye shyaamol boner chaaye
Chhorhiye galo shokol khaaney gaaney gaaney.

The sky vibrates to the roll of distant drums;
clouds loom heavy on the dark horizon.
My heart sways in rhythm to those resonant chords
and loses itself in its own music.

Where in the depths of my soul
was this secret pain,
buried deep,
in a secret harmony?

Now, when shadows are deepening in the forest
and the air dark and moist with coming rain,
that pain is shattered into fragments of song
and blown to the ends of the earth by the lashing wind.

Aaji jhorer raatey tomaar obhishaar
poraan-shokhaa bondhu hey aamaar.
Aakaash kaandey hotaash shomo, naai jey ghum noyoney momo—
duaar khuli hey priyotomo, chaai jey baarey baar.
Baahirey kichhu dekhitey naahi paai,
tomaar poth kothaay bhaabi taai.
Shudoor kone nodir paarey gohon kone boner dhaarey
gobheer kone ondhokaarey hoteychho tumi paar.

Tonight is your tryst
my beloved; my friend,
and the night is stormy and dark.

The sky weeps tears of a deep despair.
I stand by the door
and with eyes that know no sleep
gaze out into the dark.

Invisible is the world outside.
Where lies your path beloved one?
Perchance by the bank of some distant river,
crossing a weary stretch of forest wild,
in the deep darkness of this endless night.

Esho go, jweley diye jaao prodeep khaani
bijon ghorer koney, esho go.
Naamilo sraabon shondhyaa,
kaalo chhaayaa ghonaay boney boney.
Aano bishmoy momo nibhrito protikkhaay jootheemaalikaar
mridu gondhey—
neel-boshon-onchol-chhaayaa
shukhorojoni-shomo meluk money.
Haariye gachhey more baanshi,
aami kone shurey daaki tomaarey
Potho cheye-thaakaa more drishtikhaani
shunitey paao ki taahaar baanee—
kompito bokkher porosho meley ki shojol shomeeroney.

Come, light the lamp in a corner of
my solitary chamber.
The melancholy dusk of a rainy day descends;
dark shadows grow darker in the forest.

Into the secret world of my anguished yearning,
bring the wonder of your presence,
with the gentle fragrance of jasmine blossoms.

Spread the shadows of your blue veil over my heart,
like sweet nocturnal dreams.

The flute is lost on which I played.
To what strains of music shall I serenade you?

Can you hear the words unspoken by my eyes
which gaze along your path?
Can you feel in the wind, heavy with rain,
the touch of my heart trembling in ecstasy?

Money holo jano periye elem ontobiheen poth
aashitey tomaar dwaarey
moruteer hotey shudhaa shyaamolim paarey.
Potho hotey aami gaanthiyaa enechhi shikto jootheer maalaa
shokorun nibedoner gondho dhaalaa—
lojjaa diyo naa taarey.
Shojol megher chhaayaa ghonaaichhey boney boney,
Poth-haaraanor baajichhey bedonaa shomeeroney.
Door hotey aami dekhechhi tomaar oi baataayon toley
nibhritey prodeep jwoley—
Aamaar e aankhi utshuk paakhi jhorer ondhokaarey.

It seems to me that I have crossed
an endless stretch of land
to come to your door;
from the far edge of an arid desert,
to sweet green shadowy banks.

For you I have gathered
and strung into a wreath,
a cluster of moist white blooms.
Oh! spurn it not, beloved,
for in their scented depths
is buried a heart
poignant with devotion.

Heavy clouds hang their shadows
in the darkening woods.
The wind shrieks in pain
for the homeless wanderer.
From afar I can see the lamp
flickering at your casement,
and my eye, like an eager bird,
gazes upon it in the stormy dark.

Modhu-gondhey bhoraa mridu-snigdhochhaayaa neepo-kunjotoley
shyaam-kaantimoyee kone shwopnomaayaa phirey brishtijoley.
Phirey rokto-oloktoko-dhouto paaye dhaaraa-shikto baaye,
megho-mukto shohaashyo shoshaankokolaa
shinthi-praantey jwoley.
Piye uchholo torol proloymodiraa
unmukhoro-toronginee dhaaye odheeraa,
kaar nirbheek moorti torongodoley kolo mondroroley
ei taaraahaaraa nihsheem ondhokaarey kaar toroni choley.

Suffused with honey scent, soft muted shadows creep
through flowering *kadamba* groves.

Dark beauty! What illusory dreams come floating
on drifts of pelting rain?

Blood-crimson tinted feet wing by on dark moist air;
a crescent moon glimmers from a cloudless brow.

Drunk on destruction's frothing wine a restless river runs
dancing, leaping, babbling in delirium.

Swaying on waves of sonorous sound a barge;
image incarnate of gallant, intrepid life
sails through a stretch of endless, starless dark.

Shoghon gohon raatri,
jhorichhey sraabon dhaaraa—
Ondho bibhaaboree shongo porosh haaraa.
Cheye thaaki jey shunye onyo money
shethaay birohineer osru horon korechhey oi taaraa.
Oshwotho pollobey brishti jhoriyaa mormor shobdey
nisheether onidraa daaye jey bhoriyaa.
Maayaalok hotey chhaayaatoronee
bhaashaay shwopno paaraabaarey—
naahi taar kinaaraa.

The night is dense with cloud
and the showers of *Sraabon* fall.
Blinded, she gropes in silent quest
for the touch of a long-lost lover.

I gaze at that void with absent eyes
where the tears of a maid forlorn
frozen in a silver star
glimmer in the deepening gloom.

From the leaves of the peepul drip
a patter of falling rain
and a gentle murmuring rustle
fills the night's sleeplessness.

A shadowy boat comes drifting
from the lost land of illusion—
rocking on the waves of a sea of dreams
whose shores lie beyond the horizon.

Gohon raatey sraabon dhaaraa porichhey jhorey,
kano go michhey jaagaabey orey.
Ekhono duti aankhir koney jaaye jey dekhaa
joler rekhaa,
naa-bolaa baanee royechhey jano odhor bhorey.
Naa hoy jeyo gunjoriyaa beenaar taarey
moner kothaa shoyon dwaarey.
Naa hoy rekho maalotikoli shithil keshey
neerobey eshey,
naa hoy raakhi poraaye jeyo phuler dorey.
Kano go michhey jaachi jaagaabey orey.

The ceaseless torrent of a monsoon sky
fills the deep night.
Why do you wake her in vain?

Traces of tears can still be seen
in the corners of her eyes;
her lips are moist and brimming
with many words unsaid.

To the strings of your lyre
you may hum your thoughts,
at the door of her chamber.
You may come in silence,
and leave for her loosened hair,
a fragrant blossom.

You may tie the bond of love
with a garland of blooms on her slender wrist.
Why do you wake her in vain?

Aandhaaro omborey prochondo domboru
baajilo gombheero gorojoney.
Oshwottho pollobey oshaanto hillol shomeer choncholo digongoney.
Nodir kollol, boner mormoro, baadol-uchholo nirjhor jhor jhor,
dhwoni torongilo nibiro shongeetey—
sraabono shonnyashee rochilo raaginee.
Kodombokunjero shugondho modeeraa
ojosro lutichhey duronto jhotikaa.
Torit shikhaa chhutey digonto shondhiyaa,
bhoyaarto jaamini uthichhey krondiyaa—
nachichhey jano kono promotto daanobo
meghero durgero duaaro haaniyaa

In the darkening vault a mighty drum resounds;
solemn and sombre.
The leaves of the peepul sway against the sky
in passionate abandon,
as the wind comes in gusts from the lowering horizon.

The river rushes by in tumult;
a rustling is heard in the woods.
Rain clouds brimming over in joy
scatter their sparkling burden into the streams.

A great wave of sound rises from the earth
as the wild ascetic of the rains
composes a strain,
of cosmic harmony.

Fragrant pollen from the *kadamba* grove
is swept away in masses by the frenzied wind.
Streaks of lightning search the corners of the sky.
The fearful night cries out in pain
as a mighty demon drunk with power
dances against a fortress of massed clouds
battering the battlements.

Aamaar din phuraalo byaakul baadol shaanjhey
gohon megher nibir dhaaraar maajhey.
Boner chhayaay jol chholochholo shurey
hridoy aamaar kaanaay kaanaay poorey.
Kkhoney kkhoney oi guru guru taaley taaley
gogoney gogoney gobheer mridong baajey.
Kone doorer maanush jano elo aaj kaachhey,
timir aaraaley nirobey daanraaye aachhey.
Bukey doley taar biroho byaathaar maalaa
gopon-milon-omrito-gondho dhaalaa.
Money hoy taar choroner dhwoni jaani—
haar maani taar ojaanaa joner shaajey.

My day ends,
in the saddened twilight of a monsoon eve;
in the unceasing torrents
that fall from heavy clouds.

In the deepening shadows of the forest,
to the relentless melody of splashing rain,
my heart fills to the brim.

Thundering drums are heard in the distance,
echoing from sky to sky.

It seems to me,
that a stranger from an alien land,
hiding himself in the dark of night,
is very near.

On his breast sways a garland woven
with the anguished blooms of estrangement,
concealing in their depths
the fragrance of a secret reunion.

It seems to me
that I hear his footsteps
echoing in my heart
and I surrender to one,
who pretends to be a stranger.

Shwopney aamaar money holo
kokhon ghaa diley aamaar dwaarey, haay.
Aaami jaagi naai jaagi naai go,
tumi milaaley ondhokaarey, haay.
Ochetono mono-maajhey tokhon rimijhimi dhwoni baajey,
kaanpilo boner chhaayaa jhilli jhonkaarey.
Aami jaagi naai jaagi naai go, nodi bohilo boner paarey.
Pothik elo dui prohorey pother aaobhaan aani ghorey.
Shiyorey neerob beenaa bejeychhilo ki jaani naa—
jaagi naai jaagi naai go,
ghirechhilo bonogondho ghumero chaari dhaarey.

I thought in my dream that you knocked on my door
but alas! I did not awake.
You merged in the dark and I was left wailing
abandoned, desolate.

Somewhere in the depths of my soul there rang
the echoes of jewelled feet,
like the shivering shadows in the vibrant woods
when at dusk the hedge crickets sing;
but alas! I did not awake and the stream
flowed on by the murmuring trees.

In the dead of night a traveller came
with a call from a path unknown.
I know not if his hand touched the slumbering strings
of the lyre of my silent soul.
Alas! I did not awake and the scent
of the forest encircled my sleep.

Shyaamol chhaayaa, naaibaa geley
shesh boroshaar dhaaraa dheley.
Shomoy jodi phuriye thaakey—heshey bidaay koro taakey,
ebaar naa hoy kaataak belaa oshomoyer khelaa kheley.
Molin, tomaar milaabey laaj,—
shorot eshey poraabey shaaj.
Nobeen robi uthbey haashi, baajaabey megh shonaar baanshi—
kaaloy aaloy jugol roopey shuniye debey milon meley.

Dark shadow, do not go,
leaving behind you a belated stream
of tearful rain.
If your time be indeed over,
bid adieu with a smile.

Let the ragged garments of your shame
stream away with the wind.
Adorn yourself in autumn's choicest gems.
Let the new sun dazzle its light upon your face
and the clouds play symphonies on flutes of gold.

Let dark and light mingle together
in a twin vision of glory,
floating in the void,
in mutual harmony.

Shorot, tomaar orun aalor onjoli
chhoriye galo chaapiye mohon onguli.
Shorot, tomaar shishir-dhoyaa kuntoley
boner-pothey lutiye poraa oncholey
aaj probhaater hridoy othey choncholi.
Maanik-gaanthaa oi-jey tomaar konkoney
jhilik laagaay tomaar shyaamol ongoney.
Kunjochaayaa gunjoroner shongeetey
orhnaa orhaay eki naacher bhongeetey,
shiuli boner buk jey othey aandoli.

Autumn, the light of your dawn
seeps like liquid gold
through enchanted fingers.

Your tresses washed with silver dew,
your mantle trailing through the forest tracks
make the heart of the morn quiver with a
joy unknown.

Your bracelets, starred with priceless gems,
dazzle your green fields with glittering sparks.

To the humming of birds the shadows of the bower
flutter their veils in joyful dance
and sets the heart of the *shiuli* grove
swaying in abandon.

Hridoye chhiley jegey,
dekhi aaj shorot meghey
kemoney aajkey bhorey galo go galo shorey
tomaar oi aanchol khaani shishirer chhonyaa legey.
Ki jey gaan gaahitey chaai,
baanee more khunjey naa paai.
Shey jey oi shiulidoley chhoraalo kaanon toley,
shey jey oi kkhonik dhaaraay urey jaay baayu begey.

Lo! I behold you in the autumn clouds
and know that you were awake in my soul.

Your veil, touched with the dewdrops of dawn
moves gently away from my vision;
I know not where!

I know not what melody is buried in my breast;
what words can give it birth.

Perchance the fragments blew away with the wind
along with the *shiuli* flowers
that fall in red-white heaps,
on the dew drenched grass of the grove.

Shorot e aaj kone otithi elo praaner dwaarey.
Aanondogaan gaa rey hridoy, aanondogaan gaa rey.
Neel aakaasher neerob kothaa shishir bhejaa byaakulotaa.
Bejey uthuk aaji tomaar beenaar taarey taarey.
Shoshyo kkheter shonaar gaaney jog dey rey aaj shomaan taaney,
bhaashiye dey shur bhoraa nodeer omol jolodhaarey.
Jey esheychhey taahaar mukhey dakh rey cheye gobheer shukhey,
dooaar khuley taahaar shaathey baahir hoye jaa rey.

A stranger came knocking on the doors of my heart
in the dewy golden dawn.
Sing a song of elation my soul, my soul!
on this bright autumn morn.

The words unspoken by the deep blue sky—
its eager expectancy;
oh! let them ring out to the strings of your lyre
in a joyous rhapsody.

The corn fields are singing a lyric of gold;
join them with equal joy.
The river, full to the brim, sparkling pure,
will carry your strains on its crest.

Look full into the face of the one who is near;
open your doors with love.
Walk out into the world, hand in hand with the stranger,
and never glance behind.

Aakaash hotey khoshlo taaraa aandhaar raatey potho haaraa.
Probhaat taarey khunjtey jaabey—
dhoraar dhoolaay khunjey paabey
triney triney shishirdhaaraa.
Dukher pothey galo choley—niblo aalo, morlo jwoley.
Robir aalo nemey eshey miliye nebey bhaalobeshey,
dukkho tokhon hobey shaaraa.

A star came hurtling from the sky
and lost itself in the deep dark night.
The dawn will search all over the earth
and find it in the dewdrops on the grass.

The light went out, consumed by searing pain,
on the path of sorrow over which it flew.
When the sun sends down a golden ray,
melting the dew with a loving glance,
that pain will be no more.

Shorot-aalor komolboney
baahir hoye bihaar korey jey chhilo more money money.
Taari shonaar kaankon baajey aaji probhaatkiron-maajhey,
haaoaay kaanpey aancholkhaani—
chhoraay chhaayaa kkhoney kkhoney.
Aaakul kesher porimoley
shiuli boner udaash baayu porey thaakey torutoley.
Hridoy maajhey hridoy dulaay, baahirey shey bhubon bhulaay—
aaji shey taar chokher chaaoaa chhoriye dilo neel gogoney.

She who dwelt in secret,
in the depths of my soul,
reveals herself in this clear autumn light
and walks abroad in the wilderness of lilies.

In the golden rays of the dawn
her jewelled bracelets tinkle,
and her veil, fluttering in the breeze,
chequers the earth with light and shadow.

Caught by the scent of her flowing hair
the languishing wind in the *shiuli* grove
lies, fainting, under the trees.

Within, she makes my heart sway in my breast;
the world without is caught in her spell—
when she opens her eyes
and gazes upon the blue, blue sky.

Shei to tomaar pother bondhu shei to.
Door kushumer gondho eney khonjaay modhu shei to.
Shei to tomaar pother bondhu shei to.
Ei aalo taar ei to aandhaar, ei aachhey ei nei to.

It is he who is your lover;
he that waylays you on your path;
who brings you the scent of a distant bloom
and makes you long for honey.

It is he who is your lover.
This light is his, and his this dark;
brightly vivid now,
now vanished in a spark!

Heymontey kone boshonteri baanee poornoshoshee oi-jey dilo aani.
Bokul doler aagaay jyotsnaa jano phuler shwopon laagaay.
Kone gopon kaanaa kaani poornoshoshee oi jey dilo aani.
Aabesh laagey boney shwet korobeer okaal jaagoroney.
Daakchhey thaaki thaaki ghoom haaraa
kone naam-naa-jaanaa paakhi.
Kaar modhur shmoronkhaani poornoshoshee oi-jey dilo aani.

On a night of late autumn the full moon
brings a message of spring.
Its silver beams tip the boughs of the *bakul*
with flowery dreams
and waft in the mist
the music of many a secret murmur.

The woods sway in a languorous trance
as the white oleander
opens her dreaming eyes.

A bird unknown breaks the silence of the sky
in a voice throbbing with the anguish
of many a sleepless night.
Whose sweet remembrance does the full moon bring
on this night of late autumn?

Himer raatey oi gogoner deepgulirey
hemontikaa korlo gopon aanchol ghirey.
Ghorey ghorey daak paathaalo— 'deepaalikaay jwaalaao aalo,
jwaalaao aalo, aapon aalo, shaajaao aaloy dhoritreerey.'
Shunyo ekhon phuler baagaan, doyel kokil gaahey naa gaan,
kaash jhorey jaay nodeer teerey.
Jaak oboshaad bishaad kaalo, deepaalikaay jwaalaao aalo—
jwaalaao aalo, aapon aalo, shunaao aalor joybaanee rey.
Debtaaraa aaj aachhey cheye—jaago dhoraar chheley-meye,
aaloy jaagaao jaamini rey.
Elo aandhaar din phuraalo, deepaalikaay jwaalaao aalo,
jwaalaao aalo, aapon aalo, joy koro ei taamoshirey.

On a dewy night in November
the lamps burning in the sky
are hidden by a veil of mist
that the dying spirit of autumn
wraps trembling, fold by fold.

Her call resounds in every home:
Light your lamp, your soul aflame;
dazzle with light, the earth!

The gardens now are bare of blossom,
birds no longer sing;
the feathery blooms of the reeds by the river
keep falling, falling, falling.

All languor dissipate! Destroy all dark distress.
Light your lamp, your soul aflame;
let earth resound to all-conquering light!

Now, when the gods are watching from the sky,
awake oh! sons and daughters of the earth;
wake the sleeping night,
with a burst of radiance.

Dusk is flowing in; the day is almost done.
Light your lamp, your soul aflame;
vanquish this thick black night!

Sheeter boney kone shey kothin aashbey bo'ley
shiuliguli bhoye molin boner koley.
Aamloki-daal shaajlo kaangaal, khoshiye dilo pollobjaal,
kaasher haashi haaoaay bhaashi jaay jey choley.
Shoibey naa shey paataay ghaashey choncholotaa
taai to aapon rong ghuchaalo jhumkolotaa.
Uttor baay jaanaay shaashon, paatlo toper shushko aashon,
shaaj-khoshaabaar ei leela kaar ottoroley.

In the heart of the forest the few last *shiuli* blooms
tremble in their mother's lap, pale with fear.
The harsh Lord of winter is coming!

The branch of the *amloki* tree, feigning poverty,
hastily sheds its net of leaves.

The feathery fronds of the reeds let their gay laughter
float away in the wind
to the last echo.

Wrathful will he be, if he sees in the leaves and grass,
any sign of mirth or play.

So the bell flower on the creeper
disperses its blushes in the air
and grows pale and faint.

The North wind blows in threatening gusts;
all is empty and still.
With a great roar of rasping laughter,
he begins his game of stripping all gilding from the woods.

Sheeter haaoaar laaglo naachon aamlokir ei daaley daaley.
paataaguli shirshiriye jhoriye dilo taaley taaley.
Uriye debaar maaton eshey kaangaal taarey korlo sheshey,
tokhon taahaar pholer baahaar roilo naa aar ontoraaley.
Shunyo korey bhorey deoaa jaahaar khelaa
taari laagi roinu boshey shokol belaa.
Sheeter porosh thekey thekey jaay bujhi oi dekey dekey,
shob khoaabaar shomoy aamaar hobey kokhon kone shokaaley.

The winter wind dances in wild abandon,
on the branches of the *amloki* tree.
To the beat of its passionate swaying
the leaves fall, fluttering, trembling to the ground.
Drunk with the power of destruction, the blast
strips her of all her leaves.
Where can she, now her screen is gone,
hide her wealth of gleaming fruit?

Who snatches all, creating a vast void,
then piles with lavish hands until the heart is full;
for him I wait the long and dreary day.
I feel his breath, perchance, in the icy blasts,
hear in the distance, echoes of his call.
Ah! when will he come to rob me of my all?
I wait in patience for that distant morn.

Shiuli-photaa phurolo jei phurolo sheeter boney
eley jey—
aamaar sheeter boney eley jey shei shunyokkhoney.
Taai goponey shaajiye daalaa dukher shurey boronmaalaa
gaanthi money money shunyokkhoney.
Diner kolaaholey
dhaakaa shey jey roibey hridoytoley—
Raater taaraa uthbey jobey shurer maalaa bodol hobey
tokhon tomaar shoney money money.

When the last *shiuli* faded
you came;
you came to my wintry woods
in a moment of emptiness.

In secret I filled my basket of welcome,
weaving a garland with strains of sorrow
within my heart,
in a moment of emptiness.

In the noise and clamour of the day
it will lie hidden deep down in my soul;
my garland will lie hidden.

When the stars of the night rise above the horizon,
our garlands of song we will then exchange
within our hearts,
in a moment of fulfillment.

Baashonti, hey bhubonmohinee,
dik praantey bonbonaantey,
shyaam praantorey, aamrochhaaye,
shorobor teerey, nodeeneerey,
neel aakaashey, moloybaataashey
byaapilo ononto tobo maadhuri.
Nogorey graamey kaanoney, diney nisheethey,
pikshongeetey, nrityogeet koloney bishwo aanondito
bhoboney bhoboney beenaa taan rono-rono jhonkrito.
Modhumod modito hridoye hridoye rey
nobopraano uchhoshilo aaji,
bicholito chito uchholi unmaadonaa
jhon-jhon jhonilo monjirey monjirey.

Spring, enchanting Spring!

From the distant horizon, to the edge of the wood,
over green meadows, past shadows of mangoes,
by the emerald lake, over the rippling river,
suffusing blue skies, on gentle breezes,
you draw the veil of your peerless charm.

In city and village, in grove and garden,
by day, by night, to the cuckoo's call,
in song and dance, the world rejoices.

In every home your melodious lyre
rings resonant on this new morn.
In every heart, suffused with the wine
of heady youth, a new day dawns.

The restless heart on a wave of elation
to the clash of your cymbals, rings wild and free.

Spring, enchanting Spring!

Dheerey dheerey dheerey bao ogo utol haaoaa,
nisheethraater baanshi baajey—shaanto hao go shaanto hao.
Aami prodeepshikhaa tomaar laagi bhoye bhoye ekaa jaagi,
moner kothaa kaaney kaaney mridu mridu kao-o.
Tomaar doorer gaatha tomaar boner baanee
ghorer koney deho aani.
Aamar kichhu kothaa aachhey bhorer belaay taaraar kaachhey,
shei kothaati tomaar kaaney chupichupi lao.

Softly, blow softly, wild wind of the South;
in silver silence, in sweet tranquility;
now upon the midnight air a flute is heard playing
a distant melody.

I, the flame of a flickering lamp,
keep vigil for you in fear;
for you beloved, for the words of your heart
to be whispered in my ear.

Ah! bring to me in my lonely nook
your tales of far away;
the murmurings of your secret woods
by the fleeting light of day.

I, too, have a word buried in my heart,
to be told to the star at dawn;
take that in your ear in silent stealth
when fading away with the morn.

Tumi kone pothey jey eley pothik, aami dekhi naai tomaarey.
Hothaat shwopon-shomo dekhaa diley boneri kinaarey.
Phaaguney jey baan dekechhey maatir paathaarey
tomaar shobuj paaley laaglo haaoaa eley joaarey
bheshey eley joaarey—jouboner joaarey.
Kone deshey jey baashaa tomaar key jaaney thikaanaa.
Kone gaaner shurer paarey taar pother naai nishaanaa.
Tomaar shei desher i torey aamaar mon jey kemon korey—
tomaar maalaar gondhey taari aabhaash
aamaar praaney bihaarey.

Oh! traveller from a distant land,
by what path did you come?
At the edge of the wood, as if in a dream,
I saw your silent form.

Now March has brought a mighty flood
in the ocean of the land;
your green sails have caught the wind
and come floating on the tide;
youth's swiftly surging tide.

No one knows where lies your home,
nor the country of your birth.
Is it by the bank of some stream of song
to which there lies no path?

For that land of no return,
my heart is sick with love;
A lingering glimpse suffuses my soul
from the fragrance that circles your form.

Aakaash aamaay bhorlo aaloy, aakaash aami bhorbo gaaney
shurer abeer haanbo haaoaay, naacher abeer haaoaay haaney.
Orey polaash, orey, polaash,
raangaa ronger shikhaay shikhaay dikey dikey aagun jwolaash—
aamaar moner raag raaginee raangaa holo rongeen taaney.
Dokhin-haaoaay kushum boner buker kaanpon thaamey naa jey.
Neel aakaashey shonaar aaloy kochi paataar noopur baajey.
Orey shireesh orey shireesh,
mridu haashir ontoraaley gondhojaaley shunyo ghirish—
tomaar gondho aamaar konthey aamaar hridoy teney aney.

The sky fills me with light,
I shall fill the sky with song.
I shall spray upon the dancing winds
bright hues of melody!

Flame of the forest! my forest flame!
your fiery tongues leap vaulting, dancing,
darting, passion all embracing;
dyeing the strains of my soul's music
in a crimson harmony.

The South wind blows in a forest of flowers;
heart's tremble does not cease—
in the deep blue sky, in the golden light
young leaves tinkle their jewelled feet.

Ah raintree green and misty gold!
Concealed by a screen of gentle laughter
you breathe into the waiting void
a net of perfume, cloying, clinging;
making my heart sing in my throat
a crooning, throbbing symphony.

Ektuku chhonyaa laagey, ektuku kothaa shuni—
taai diye money money rochi momo phaalgunee.
Kichhu polaasher neshaa, kichhu baa chaampaay meshaa,
taai diye shurey shurey rongey roshey jaal buni.
Jetuku kaachhetey aashey kkhoniker phaankey phaankey
chokito moner koney shwoponer chhobi aankey.
Jetuku jaay re doorey bhaabnaa kaanpaay shurey,
taai niye jaay belaa noopurer taal guni.

A little touch like a gentle breeze,
a little word heard from afar;
with these I weave a fantasy
of a silver moon in spring.

The flame of the forest yields a spray
of crimson coloured wine,
mixed with the scent of the golden dust
from the fainting *champa* flying;
with these I weave a sensuous web
of melody, colour and light.

The fragment that comes floating
on a moment's broken wing,
paints a dream of startled bliss
in a corner of my being.

That which moves far, far away
on the trembling waves of song;
with that I pass the livelong day,
counting the beat of jewelled feet.

O aamaar chaander aalo, aaj phaaguner shondhyaakaaley
dhoraa diyechho jey aamaar paataay paataay daaley daaley.
Jey gaan tomaar shurer dhaaraay
bonyaa jaagaay taaraay taaraay
more aanginaay baajlo go,
baajlo shey-shur aamaar praaner taaley taaley.
Shob kunri more phutey othey tomaar haashir ishaaraatey.
Dokhin-haaoaa dishaahaaraa aamaar phuler gondhey maatey.
Shubhro tumi korley bilole—
Aamaar praaney ronger hilole
mormorito mormo go,
mormo aamaar joraay tomaar haashir jaaley.

What gentle surrender
ah! moonlight, my moonlight,
in the spring leaves and branches
of my trees in the twilight.

What wave of wild rapture
from the stream of your song
washes with silver
the stars of the night.

The same tune that rings
with a thrill on my threshold,
to the beat of my heart;
to the throb of my soul.

My buds all awaken
at your beckoning smile;
At the scent of my blossoms
the South wind goes wild.

Ah! white, with a splash,
a riot of colours,
you trap my soul's yearning
in the web of your smile.

Choley jaay mori haay boshonter din.
Door shaakhey pik daakey biraam biheen.
Odheer shomeer-bhorey uchhoshi bokul jhorey,
gondho-shoney holo mon shudoorey bileen.
Pulokito aamrobeethi phaalguneri taapey,
modhukor gunjoroney chhaayaatol kaanpey.
Kano aaji okaaroney shaaraa belaa aanmoney
poraaney baajaay beenaa key go udaasheen.

Ah me!
Soft balmy days will be no more
for spring is going fast;
the cuckoo, ceaseless, trills her tunes
from a far-off leafy branch.

White *bakul* float like starry flakes
on the fevered, restless, wind;
carrying my heart to a distant land
in a cloud of heady scent.

Shivers of thrill in the mango grove
at the first warm winds of March,
make shadows flicker in the vernal woods;
bees hum from flowery perch.

On this new morn I feel the touch
of someone's careless hand
plucking the strings, I know not why,
of the lyre of my languid heart.

Songs of Many Moods

এই
আমার ছোটো খানি [illegible]
সারা সকাল পেতে রাখি
ঝরনা ধারার নিচে। বসে থাকি একটি ধারে
শেওলা-ঢাকা পিছল কালো পাথরগুলোর [illegible]।
ঘট ভরে যায় বারে বারে
ফেনিয়ে ওঠে, ছাপিয়ে [illegible] পড়ে [illegible], কিনারি,।
সবুজ দিয়ে [illegible] ঝিলে-মিলে
শৈল শ্রেণীর [illegible] নীল আকাশে [illegible]
দিনে রাতে।
ঝরঝরানির মাঝে ওঠে [illegible]

ভোরের ঘুমে ডাক শোনে তার
জলের শব্দ [illegible] গাঁয়ের মেয়েরা।
[illegible] যায় কোথা সে
কোন্ বহুদূর নদীর সীমানায়;
পাহাড়তলীর [illegible] রাস্তা ছেড়ে [illegible] যেখানে ঐ হাটের মানুষ
ধীরে ধীরে উঠছে চড়াই পথে
বলদ জুটির [illegible] পিঠে [illegible] বোঝাই
শুকনো কাঠের [illegible]। রুনুঝুনু ঘন্টা গলায় বাঁধা।
ঐ [illegible] আকাশ ছাপিয়ে
[illegible] তারপর তোমার উদাসীন, কিছু কোথায় চলে
[illegible]। অর্থহারা সুরে বিজন,

রাস্তা দিয়ে সকাল বেলার প্রথম রোদের রং,
উঠল আঁকা হয়ে।
ফিকে ধূসর পাহাড় ছাড়িয়ে।
চুপ করে সব শুনি,
বেলা গেলো, ডাক পাড়ে যারা।
ঘট ভরতে হয় না দেরি [illegible] — ওরা আমায় [illegible], রাগ করে কয়
সবাই তোরে, [illegible] দেরী কেমন বেল,
উপচে পড়া জলের কথা [illegible] [illegible],
বুঝিনে না তো [illegible]।

E shudhu olosho maayaa, e shudhu meghero khelaa,
e shudhu monero shaadh baataasheytey bishorjon.
E shudhu aapon money maalaa genthey chhinrey phelaa,
nimesher haashi kaannaa gaan geye shomaapon.
Shyaamol pollobopaatey robikorey shaaraa belaa
aaponaari chaayaa loye khelaa korey phulguli—
eo shei chhaayaakhelaa boshontero shomironey.
Kuhoker deshey jano shaadh korey poth bhuli
hethaa hothaa ghuri phiri shaaraa din aanmoney.
Kaarey jano debo bo'ley kothaa jano phul tuli—
shondhyaay molin phul urey jaay boney boney.
E khelaa khelibey, haay, khelaar shaathi ke aachhey.
Bhuley bhuley gaan gaai—key shoney, key naai shoney—
Jodi kichhu money porey, jodi keho aashey kaachhey.

Only idle illusion,
only the play of clouds,
only heart's desire
released in the streaming wind.
This is only the weaving and tearing
of garlands in seclusion;
the tears and laughter of moments
concluded with a song.

The beams of the sun fall slanting
on fringes of green leaves;
with their shadows fleet, the flowers sweet
play, in the golden eve:
the self same sport of light and shade,
played by the winds of spring.

In a land of enchantment I lose my path
in joyous willful surrender.
I pluck a flower in my wanderings
for one; I know not who!
At dusk the wilting bloom is blown
away to the forest dim.

Will you play this game? Alas!
Who will your playmate be?
I sing in sheer forgetfulness.
Who hears? Who does not hear?
If something I remember;
if someone comes to me!

Dekhaa naa-dekhaay meshaa hey bidyutlotaa,
kaanpaao jhorer bukey eki byaakulotaa.
Gogoney shey ghurey ghurey khonjey kaachhey, khonjey doorey—
Shohoshaa ki haashi haasho, naahi jaaney naam,
ki rudro shondhaaney shindhu dulichhey durdaam.
Oronyo hotaashopraaney aakaashey lolaato haaney,
dikey dikey kendey pherey ki duhshoho byaathaa.

A lightning creeper flashes a trail of gold;
now seen, now invisible
and the heart of the storm quivers with
unbearable longing.

To the ends of the sky he flies in search;
now near, now far away,
beguiled by a burst of sudden laughter
but not a spoken word.

Dark grows the void; the mighty ocean swells—
now high, now low in fury,
in terrible quest of one whose name he does not know.

The forest in dark dejection dashes its head
against the sky;
now here, now to the far horizon
it wends its moaning way in unbearable anguish.

Gogoner thaaley robi chondro deepok jwoley,
Taarokaamondol chomokey moti rey.
Dhoop moloyaanil, pobon chaamor korey,
shokol bonoraaji phulonto jyoti rey.
Kamon aaroti, hey bhobokhondon, tobo aaroti—
onaahoto shobdo baajonto bheri rey.

In the sky's platter
the sun and moon have lighted lamps;
pearls gleam from a star spangled dark.

The air, blue as incense smoke,
waves like a fan brush
and beams burst from the heavens
like a forest in bloom.

What greetings are these
that earth shattering rebounds?
What unstruck drums
beat out this volley of sounds?

Naa go, ei jey dhulaa aamaar naa e.
Tomaar dhulaar dhoraar porey
uriye jaabo shondhyaa baaye.
Diye maati aagun jwaali rochley deho poojaar thaali—
Shesh aaroti shaaraa k'orey bhengey jaabo tomaar paaye.
Phul jey chhilo poojaar torey
jetey pothey daali hotey onek jey taar gachhey porey.
Koto prodeep ei thaalaatey shaajiyechhiley aapon haatey—
koto jey taar niblo haaoaay, pounchholo naa choronchhaaye.

No, this is not mine, this dust.
Over the dust of your earth
what is yours I must scatter
now, upon this evening air.

From out of the furnace the clay emerged;
the created body—vessel of God;
the last rite over, at your feet I will shatter
now, upon this evening air.

Many a flower that were for your worship
dropped from my basket upon the path.
Many a lamp lit with loving hands,
ere they reached the shadows of your peerless feet,
a gust of wind and they flickered and faded
now, upon this evening air.

Aamraa nooton jouboneri doot
aamraa chonchol, aamraa odbhut.
Aamraa beraa bhaangi,
aamraa oshokeboner raangaa neshaay raangi.
Jhonjhaar bondhon chhinno korey dii—aamraa bidyut.
Aamraa kori bhul—
ogaadh joley jhaanp diye jujhiye paai kool.
Jekhaaney daak porey jeebon-moron-jhorey
aamraa prostut.

From the flaming blossoms
of a wild wood in spring,
we drink the fiery wine.
We burst the storm's shackles
with a flash of blue lightning.
We are restless, we are strange;
we who are the heralds
of the new youth.

We plunge into the torrent;
we make many a mistake
but struggling with the current
we find our resting place.
Wherever we are needed,
in a life and death struggle,
we are ever ready;
we who are the heralds
of the new youth.

Jwol jwol chitaa, dwigun dwigun—
poraan shompibey bidhobaa baalaa.
Jwoluk jwoluk chitaar aagun,
juraabey ekhoni praaner jwaalaa.

Shone rey jobon, shone rey toraa,
je jwaalaa hridoye jwaalaali shobey
saakshi ro'len debotaa taar—
er protiphol bhugitey hobey.

Dakh rey jogot, meliye noyon,
dakh rey chondromaa, dakh rey gogon,
shworgo hotey shob dakho debogon—
jwolod-okkhorey raakho go likhey.

Spordhito jobon, toraa o dakh rey,
shotitwo-roton koritey rokkhon.
Raajput-shoti aajikey kamon
shompichhey poraan onolshikhey.

Burn pyre burn, leap double fold!
Embrace in your flames this widowed lass.
Burn fire burn, with all your might
and quench the thirst of a searing soul.

Hear oh infidel! hear oh hear!
Her God bears witness to the flaring torch
you set alight in her tender breast.
In the same blaze your heart will scorch.

See oh Earth—your eyes wide open.
Observe oh Moon and boundless sky.
Witness oh gods from your seats in heaven
and write your will in flowing words.

Bold infidel, arrogant, audacious,
with blinded eyes from blood and lust!
Behold a Rajput shield the gem
she prizes above a pitiful life.
The gem of chastity she bears within her
and flings in the flames of a glowing pyre.

O jonaaki, ki shukhey oi daanaa duti meleychho.
Aandhaar shaanjhey boner maajhey ullaashey praan dheleychho.
Tumi no o to shoorjo, no o to chondro,
tomaar taai boley ki kom aanondo.
Tumi aapon jeebon poorno korey aapon aalo jwelechho.
Tomaar jaa aachhey taa tomaar aachhey,
tumi no o go hrinee kaaro kaachhey,
tomaar ontorey jey shokti aachhey taari aadesh pelechho.
Tumi aandhaar baandhon chhariye otho,
tumi chhoto hoye no o go chhoto,
jogotey jethaay joto aalo shobaay aapon ko'rey phelechho.

Dotting the darkness
in the twilight gloaming,
your joyous wings a-flutter
your heart o'er brimming,
your twinkle ah! glow worm,
bright pin point of gold,
lights up the forest.

You have not the sun's beams
nor the radiance of the moon;
your happiness glowing
like a jewel in the gloom,
springs from the glory
of a life fulfilled.

What is yours you share,
beholden to none;
your power from within
lights a lamp in the dusk.

Not for you the bonds
of a fathomless dark.
Obscure though you are
you are vanquished by none
for all the light of the world,
you have conquered and won
with your gentle twinkle.
Ah! happy glow worm.

Hey aakaash bihaari-nirodebaahon jol,
aachhilo shoilo shikhorey-shikhorey tomaar leelaasthol
Tumi boroney boroney kironey kironey,
praatey shondhyaay oruney hironey
diyechho bhaashaay poboney poboney shwopon toronidol.
Sheyshey shyaamol maatir premey tumi bhuley eshechhiley nemey,
kobey baandhaa porey geley jekhaaney dhoraar gobheer timirtol.
Aaj paashaan dooaar diyechhi tutiyaa,
koto jug porey esheychho chhutiyaa
Neel gogoner haaraano shmoron
gaaneytey shomuchhol.

Long long ago, on mountain peaks,
dissolved in silver vapour,
cloud borne, aloft on the vast dim sky
you danced in dalliance gay.

On the wings of roving winds a fleet
of dream boats you set sail,
when the sky at dusk stood sunset flushed;
in the morn's gold radiance.

Then passionate love with the emerald earth
o'ertook you in your dreams,
and knowing not, you would be caught,
flew down on silver wings.

In a giant vault, deep, dark as night,
you lay enslaved, alone,
till with a song I burst the dykes;
the towering walls of stone.

Faint misty memory of clear blue sky,
today from fear set free
float in your eyes with the strains of my song
in swelling ecstasy.

Oi jaanaalaar kaachhey boshey aachhey
korotoley raakhi maathaa—
taar koley phul porey royechhey,
shey jey bhuley gachhey maalaa gaanthaa.
Shudhu jhuru jhuru baayu bohey jaaye
taar kaaney kaaney ki jey kohey jaaye—
taai aadho shuye aadho boshiye
bhaabitechhey koto kothaa.
Chokher uporey megh bheshey jaaye, urey urey jaaye paakhi—
Shaaraa din dhorey bokuler phul
jho'rey porey thaaki thaaki.
Modhur aalosh, modhur aabesh, modhur mukher haashiti—
modhur shwoponey praaner maajhaarey
baajichhey modhur baanshiti.

She sits by the window
cheek resting on one hand.
Her lap is strewn with *bakul* flowers;
her garland lies unwoven.

Soft breezes swish and rustle past
her half reclining form.
What do they whisper in her ear?
What words unheard? What flitting thoughts?
With them she spends the live long day ...
her garland lying unwoven.

Clouds glide before her dewy eyes;
birds go winging by.
All day long the falling blooms
waft gently on a sigh.

Sweet languor wraps her slender form;
a drowsy indolence ...
a honeyed smile plays on her lips
that speaks of distant dreams ...
of a heart in which a secret flute
plays a wondrous symphony.

Din guli more shonaar khaanchaay roilo naa—
shei-jey aamaar naanaa ronger din guli.
Kaannaa haashir baandhon taaraa shoilo naa—
shei-jey aamaar naanaa ronger din guli.
Aamaar praaner gaaner bhaashaa
shikhbey taaraa chhilo aashaa—
urey galo, shokol kothaa koilo naa—
shei jey aamaar naanaa ronger din guli.
Shwopon dekhi, jano taaraa kaar ashey
pherey aamaar bhaangaa khaanchaar chaar paashey—
shei jey aamaar naanaa ronger din guli.
Eto bedon hoy ki phaanki oraa ki shob chhaayaar paakhi.
Aakaash-paarey kichhui ki go boilo naa—
shei jey aamaar naanaa ronger din guli.

I thought I could keep my rainbow coloured days
trapped in a cage of gold,
but alas! they would not bear the strain,
the bonds of tears and laughter.
Spreading their wings away they flew;
my rainbow coloured days.

I hoped that they would learn to speak
the language of my heart,
but all in vain; they would not sing
a note of what they heard.

Sometimes I dream I see them
fluttering in the dark;
beating their wings in some fond hope
against my broken cage.

Can so much anguish be in vain?
Are they not birds but shadows?
Did nothing stream across the sky?
My rainbow coloured days?

Aalo aamaar, aalo ogo, aalo bhubon-bhoraa,
aalo noyon dhoaa aamaar,
aalo hridoy horaa.
Naachey aalo naachey, o bhaai, aamaar praaner kaachhey—
baajey aalo baajey, o bhaai, hridoy beenaar maajhey—
Jaagey aakaash, chhotey baataash, haashey shokol dhoraa.
Aalor srotey paal tulechhey haajaar projaapoti.
Aalor dheu e uthlo nechey mollika maaloti.
Meghey meghey shonaa, o bhaai, jaay naa maanik gonaa—
paataay paataay haashi, o bhaai, pulok raashi raashi—
shuronodir kool dubeychhey shudhaa-nijhor jhoraa.

This light is mine; this light that fills the world.
Dancing light! oh ringing light!
Which floods the eye, vanquishing the heart,
and plays upon the lyre of life.

The sky wakes to radiance; swift breezes blow.
The smiling earth looks on.
In the stream of light a sail unfurls
of a thousand winged moths;
and in the waves of light
sweet blossoms dance.

Clouds gleam with gold and a myriad sparkling gems.
Green leaves are touched with laughter;
with joy that knows no bounds.
The banks of the stream of melody
are washed by a flood of nectar,
flowing, sparkling light.

Toreetey paa dii ni aami, paarer paaney jaai ni go.
Ghaatei boshey kaataai belaa, aar kichhu to chaai ni go.
Toraa jaabi raajaar purey onek doorey,
toder rother chaakaar shurey
aamaar shaarhaa paai ni go.
Aamaar e jey gobheer joley kheyaa baaoaa,
hoyto kokhon nishut raatey uthbey haaoaa.
Aashbey maajhi o paar hotey ujaan srotey,
shei aashaa tei cheye aachhi—toree aamaar baai ni go.

I did not step into my boat.
I did not move towards the shore.
I spent all day sitting on the bank
asking nothing more.

You travel to a glorious land,
the city of a king, far far away;
but the echoes of your chariot wheels
make not answer to my call.

My boat is anchored in waters deep,
waiting for the wind to rise.

Perchance on some dark stormy night
against the straining tide,
my boatman comes from the distant shore
to row me out to sea.
In that fond hope I bide my time
fixing my gaze upon the deep.

Bhaango baandh bhengey daao, baandh bhengey daao,
baandh bhengey daao.
Bondi praan mon hok udhaao.
Shukno gaangey aashuk
jiboner bonyaar uddaam koutuk—
bhaangoner joygaan gaao.

Jeerno puraaton jaak bheshey jaak,
jaak bheshey jaak, jaak bheshey jaak.
Aamraa shunechhi oi maa bhoih maa bhoih maa bhoih
kone nootoneri daak.
Bhoy korinaa ojaanaarey,
ruddho taahaari dwaarey durdaarh begey dhaao.

Batter all barriers; break, break, break.
Vanish, mind and soul enslaved!
Let tumultuous laughter burst the banks
of the arid stream on a torrent of life.
Sing an anthem of destruction.
Shatter all shackles.
Break, break, break.

Let old and worn be swept away;
washed away on this new tide
of swiftly surging youth.
We have heard on the wind a clarion call
Cast out dread! From fear be free!
the call of heady youth.

We hold no terror of the strange unknown
but upon its mighty gates,
we rush headlong in battle brave.
Batter all barriers; break, break, break.

Jey kebol paaliye beraay, drishti eraay, daak diye jaay ingitey,
shey ki aaj dilo dhoraa gondhey bhoraa boshonter ei shongeetey.
O ki taar uttoreeyo oshoke shaakhaay uthlo duli
aaji ki polaashboney oi shey bulaay ronger tuli.
O ki taar choron porhey taaley taaley mollikaar oi bhongeetey.
Naa go naa, daye ni dhoraa, haashir bhoraa
deerghoshwaashey jaay bheshey.
Michhey ei helaa-dolaay mon key bholaay,
dheu diye jaay shwopney shey.
Shey bujhi lukiye aashey bichhederi rikto raatey,
noyoner aaraaley taar nityo-jaagaar aashon paatey—
Dheyaaner bornochhotaay byaathaar rongey
mon key shey roy rongitey.

Who beckons in silence beyond the reach
of human sight;
who darts away mercurial, swift,
in an endless game of hide and seek.
Is it he, held captive in this fragrant song
of melodious spring?

Is that his garment streaming in the wind,
fluttering white in the crimson blooms
flooding the branch of the *ashoka* tree?
Is it he who sprays the flame of the forest
with colours of fire?

No, no, not he, he floats away
on the laughter laden sigh of the air.
Oh! all for nothing this swaying of the heart,
these surging waves of rapturous dreams.

He comes in secret filling the void
of a night estranged;
keeps constant vigil far from the reach
of human eyes,
and colours the soul with the tranquil shades
of a pain divine.

Shohey naa jaatonaa
dibosho goniyaa goniyaa biroley
Nishidin boshey aachhi shudhu poth paaney cheye—
shokhaa hey, eleynaa.
Shohey naa jaatonaa.
Din jaaye, raat jaaye, shob jaaye—
Aami boshey haaye !
Dehey bol naai, chokhey ghum naai—
Shukaaye giyaachhey aankhijol.
Ekey ekey shob aashaa jho'rey jho'rey po'rey jaaye—
shohey naa jaatonaa.

Unbearable this anguish!
This lonesome counting of days;
this passing of the hours gazing on your path.
You come not ... my friend.

The day wanes as does the night.
All things wane.
Only I remain,
strength ebbed from limbs, eyes robbed of sleep;
tears dried on lashes,
hopes wilted and withered
but alas!
You come not ... my friend.

Ogo, toraa key jaabi paarey.
Aami tori niye boshey aachhi nodikinaarey.
O paareytey upoboney
koto khelaa koto joney,
e paaretey dhoo dhoo moru baari binaa rey.
Ei belaa belaa aachhey, aay key jaabi.
Michhey kano kaatey kaal koto ki bhaabi.
Shurjyo paatey jaabey nemey,
shubaataash jaabey themey,
kheyaa bondho hoye jaabey shondhyaa-aandhaarey.

Ah! come, who will cross to the other bank.
I wait with my boat by the side of the stream.

The forest of flowers on the distant shore
is gay with laughter, song and play,
but here is only a barren stretch
of rainless, arid waste.

While daylight still lingers in the sky,
come, who will cross to the other bank!

Soon the sun will dip in the west;
sweet breezes will cease to blow;
the ferry will close in the gloaming,
and the sky will darken with the gathering dusk.

Aaj taaraay taaraay deepto shikhaar ogni jwoley
nidraabiheen gogon toley.
Oi aaloke-maataal shworgo shobhaar mohaangon
hethaay chhilo kone jugey more nimontron—
Aamaar laaglo naa mon laaglo naa,
taai kaaler shaagor paari diye elem cho'ley
nidraabiheen gogontoley.
Hethaa mondomodhur kaanaakaani joley stholey
shyaamol maatir dhoraatoley.
hethaa ghaashey ghaashey rongeen phuler aalimpon,
boner pothey aandhaar-aaloy aalingon—
Aamaar laaglo rey mon laaglo rey,
taai ei khaaneytei din kaatey ei khelaar chholey
shyaamol maatir dhoraatoley.

In the stars tonight, bright flames of fire glow
beneath the sleepless sky.

Aeons ago, in some distant time, I went by invitation
to a great assembly in the courts of heaven
dazzled with celestial light.

But sorely did my heart ache in that strange
and distant land;
so, crossing the seas of time I came back home
beneath the sleepless sky.

Here are soft murmurings between the sea and land
upon our own green earth.
Here grass is gay with patterns of bright flowers
and in the forest tracks
light and shade embrace.

And sweetly does my heart sing in this dear familiar land,
thus, here I spend my days in this pretended play;
upon my own green earth.

Shudhu jaaoaa aashaa, shudhu srotey bhaashaa,
shudhu aalo-aandhaarey kaandaa-haashaa.
Shudhu dekhaa paaoaa, shudhu chhunye jaaoaa,
shudhu doorey jetey jetey kendey chaaoaa
shudhu nobo duraashaay aagey cho'le jaay—
pichhey pheley jaay michhey aashaa.
Oshesho baashonaa loye bhaangaa bol,
praanopon kaajey paay bhaangaa phol,
bhaangaa tori dhorey bhaashey paaraabaarey,
bhaab kendey morey—bhaangaa bhaashaa.
Hridoye hridoye aadho porichoye,
aadhkhaani kothaa shaango naahi hoy,
laajey bhoye traashey aadho-bishwaashey
shudhu aadhkhaani bhaalobaashaa.

Only to come and go,
drift gently with the tide,
Only to laugh and weep,
in a world of dark and light.
Only to catch a glimpse,
touch gently and pass on,
look back with streaming eyes,
from a long and weary road.
Only to keep moving,
spurred by vain desire.
Only to leave behind,
a trace of a hopeless hope.

When shattered strength is driven by
infinite desire;
spend all your might in labour,
broken are the fruits.
A tattered bark floats aimless
upon a mighty sea.
The soul weeps in tortured silence
and speaks in broken words.

Two hearts, half know each other;
speak half a syllable
in shame, in fear, in partial trust;
in a fragment of true love.

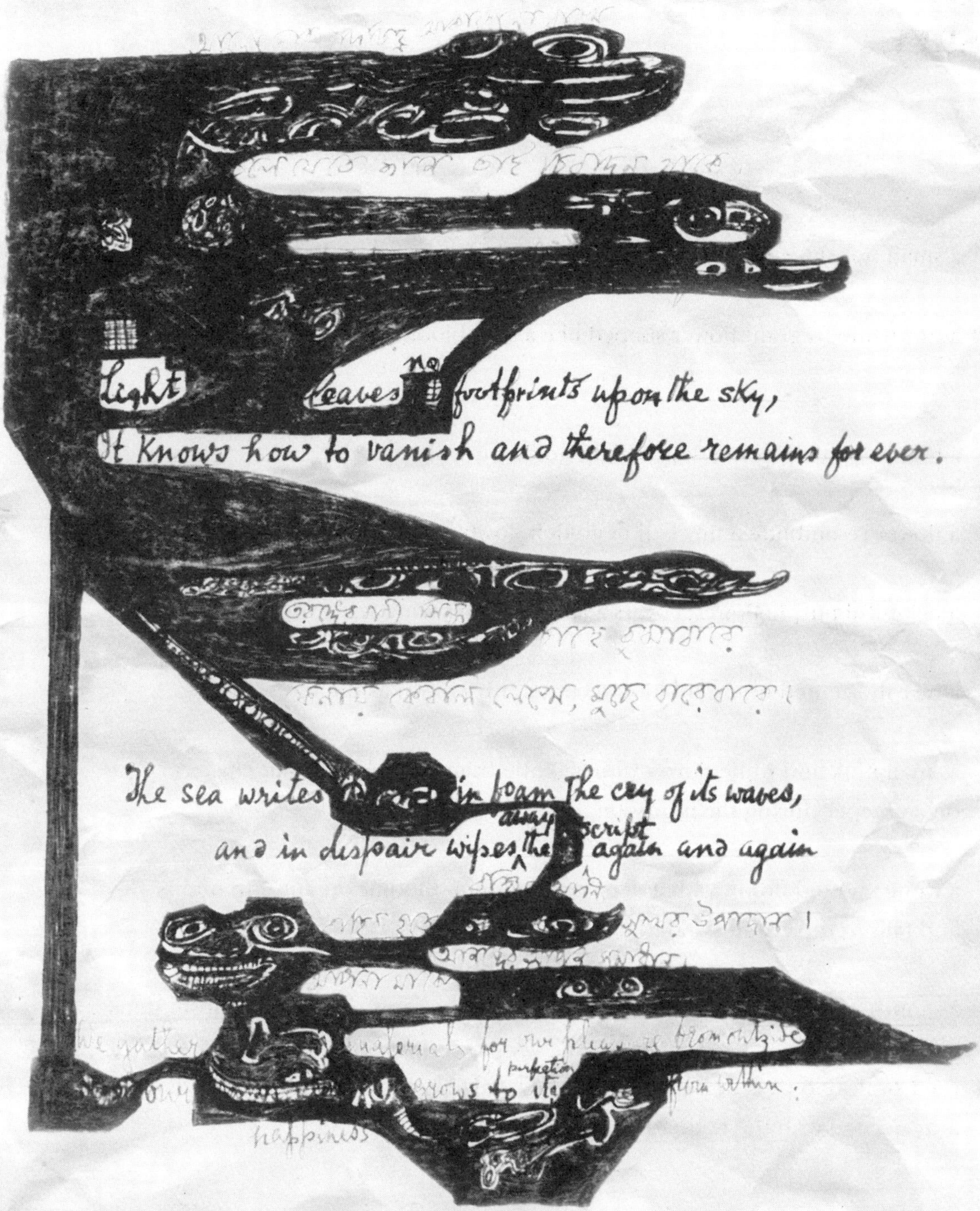
Light leaves no footprints upon the sky,
It knows how to vanish and therefore remains for ever.
The sea writes in foam the cry of its waves,
and in despair wipes away the script again and again

Glossary

amloki: a small translucent jade-green fruit; hangs in bunches on a large tree in winter.

bakul: a tiny white fragrant flower shaped like a star; blooms in spring.

champa or
champak: a highly-scented spring flower, light golden in colour.

kadamba: a flower resembling a tiny ball of golden down; blooms during the monsoon.

kanchan: a beautiful purple flower; covers a large tree in spring.

keya: a heavily scented monsoon bloom commonly known as the screwpine.

malati: a small pink and white flower with a gentle fragrance. Appears in clusters on a creeper during the monsoon.

shiuli: a white scented flower with a deep orange stem. Blooms on autumn nights and falls to the ground at dawn.

sraabon: a month in the Indian calendar during which the monsoon is at its most intense.

tamaal: the Coralwood tree; in Bengali it is called *Rakta kambal*. The tree with a dense foliage, is associated with the Radha-Krishna mythology.

Index of first lines

Songs of Love 41 - 64

Preserve in your memory
(Ei kothaati money rekho)

I shall lure you not with my beauty
(Aami roopey tomaay bholaabo naa)

You have filled the vessel of my life
(Amaar jeebon paatro uccholiyaa)

Clouds hang heavy in the twilit sky
(Aaji godhoolilogoney ei baadol gogoney)

I know you lovely alien
(Aami chini go chini tomaarey ogo bideshinee)

Make me your lyre!
(Aaamaarey koro tomaar beenaa)

On this wild night the lashing wind
(Jhorey jaaye urey jaaye go aamaar)

You shall dwell in the depths of my heart,
(Tumi robey nirobey hridoye momo)

When monsoon clouds trail shadows over the earth
(Megh chhaye shojol baaye mon aamaar)

Ah me! in this game of love with you
(Aaha, tomaar shongey praaner khelaa)

Someone has stolen the song from my throat
(Aamaar kontho hotey gaan ke nilo bhulaaye)

Seeking whom did you come with the early dawn
(Hey khoniker otithi)

I have spent my days singing by the path
(Aashaa jaaoyaar pother dhaarey)

Now that the hour of parting is near
(Aamaar jaabaar belaaye pichhu daakey)

At wane of day I fill my bark
(Dinaantobelaay shesher phoshol nilem toree-'paarey)

I have made you my lodestar
(Tomaarei koriyaachi jeeboner dhrubotaaraa)

I have not seen him yet
(Ekhono taarey chokhey dekhini)

I know not whose lyre
(Baajilo kaahaar beenaa modhur shworey)

If I knew the cause of my pain
(Jodi jaantem aamar kisher byaathaa)

Friend, dear friend!
(Olo shoi, olo shoi, aamaar ichhey)

I have felt your message within my heart
(Hey shokhaa, barotaa peyechhi money money)

Remember me
(Tobu money rekho jodi doorey jaai choley)

Songs of the Motherland 65 - 79

Leader of the masses
(Jonogonomono odhinaayok joyo hey)

A new day dawns
(Orey, nooton juger bhorey)

The tighter they tie our limbs
(Oder baandhon jotoi shokto hobey)

Turn not bewilderment into a source of humiliation
(Shonkocher bihbholotaa nijeyrey opomaan)

If no one answers to your call
(Jodi tor daak shuney keu naa aashey)

We're here together at our Mother's call
(Aamraa mileychhi aaj maayer daakey)

Do you believe you have the power
(Bidhir baandhon kaatbey tumi emon shoktimaan)